The Best Of Novel Advice

This book is a celebration, a triumph over the limitations of distance, a testimonial to the power of the Internet to unite writers from all over the world toward a common goal.

≋ Jeanne Marie Childe, Editor

NA

Novel Advice Press

PUBLISHED IN 2002 BY NOVEL ADVICE PRESS

Cover designed by Dave Workman

Text designed and typeset by
Jacqueline Jones at
Syllables, Hartwick, New York, USA

Printed and bound in the USA.

ISBN 0-9674409-0-4
LIBRARY OF CONGRESS CONTROL NUMBER: 2002117012

Editorial Sales Rights and Permission Inquiries should be addressed to:
Novel Advice Press, P.O. Box 131956, The Woodlands, TX 77393-1956

Manufactured in the United States of America

Acknowledgements

NovelAdvice.com is a Web site where serious writers gather to learn to improve their craft. Novel Advice offers courses on various aspects of the craft, an open Message Board where writers can give and receive advice, a Critique Board, a Tip of the Day, a Research Resource area, a Bookstore linked to Amazon.com, frequent contests, and our flagship Cyber-Journal, now monthly, moving soon into its eighth year of publication. Over 200 writers and 3500 articles have been published in the Cyber-Journal since it began.

Thirty writers contributed to *The Best of Novel Advice*. Their essays were selected from the nearly 1000 that appeared in the NovelAdvice Cyber-Journal in its first 30 months on the Internet. I am grateful to all the writers who agreed to be included in this anthology, especially to Caro Clarke, Elizabeth Delisi, Janis Holm, Rodney Merrill, Sunnye Tiedemann, and Eileen Alcorn Workman, each of whom contributed six or more articles, and to David Workman, who designed the cover.

I deeply appreciate the relationship I have with the folks at Syllables: Curt Akin and Jacqueline Jones. Curt, our Webmaster, is an experienced typesetter whose technical hand-holding during the early months of this project gave me the confidence to continue, despite several setbacks. Jackie Jones did the actual typesetting this fall. She chose the page design, font, and spacing, as well as the excerpts at the beginning of each article. Neither this anthology nor NovelAdvice itself would exist without their professional and personal support.

My thanks go to Lin Mouat for all she does for NovelAdvice. We would have neither a Bookstore nor a Research Resource area without her hard work. To my knowledge, Lin and I are the only two people involved with NovelAdvice who have met in person. Several years ago, Lin accompanied her husband on a business trip to the city where I lived at the time and over lunch, we forged a friendship that has stood us both in good stead.

Jacqueline Jones and Christie Gutoski assisted with proofreading copy. Janis Holm kindly responded to my questions about the basics of creating an anthology. In the end, however, I had to make my own choices and all errors are my own.

This anthology is a celebration, a triumph over the limitations of distance, a testimonial to the power of the Internet to unite writers from all over the world toward a common goal.

I am honored to be part of this endeavor.

—Jeanne Marie Childe
The Woodlands, Texas
December, 2002

http://www.noveladvice.com
jeannewrtr@noveladvice.com

TABLE OF CONTENTS

NOVEL STRUCTURE
Beginnings, Middles, Ends

Structure, Style & Voice

Settings

Needless Words

CHARACTERIZATION
Description

HUMOR

GENRE WRITING
Historical

Mystery

CREATIVE NONFICTION

MARKETING

NUTS AND BOLTS
Punctuation/Grammar

Editing & Revising

CRITICISM/REJECTION

REFERENCES

AUTHORS' BIOGRAPHIES

RECOMMENDED READING

Novel

Structure

Beginnings, Middles, Ends

Where To Start?

by Caro Clarke

*T*he opening scene of your novel should really be the opening scene. A novel is a window, opened to let us watch an arc of action from its initial to its closing phase. If you open the window too early, your readers have to drum their mental fingers while waiting for the action to start. Open the window too late, and you'll find yourself desperately filling in with flashbacks and info dumps.

How do you know which action is the initial action? What is your story about? A young girl, suffocated by small-town life, deciding to head for the big city? Or a businessman at the end of his tether who learns that, on top of everything else, he has cancer? Where do you start telling that story?

Too often the temptation is to begin by describing the people and setting the scene for your readers, so we'll understand the subsequent behavior of your characters. Thus you have the young woman rant to a friend about the constrictions on her life, or you show the businessman's hectic treadmill existence for two dozen pages to make sure we soak up its horror—in short, you spell everything out. You do this because you are worried that we, the readers, won't understand, that we are too narratively naive to grasp what's going on unless it's explained to us in baby language.

Don't worry. We *will* understand this young woman if we see her suddenly strip off her waitress's apron, announce, "I ain't taking another single minute of this," grab her day's wages, phone her clinging mother and her no-hope boyfriend, head for the Greyhound bus terminal, and be on her way to Manhattan within the hour. Later, as you show her tentatively spreading her wings in Manhattan, we will grasp what her earlier life must have been like with greater poignancy than any amount of introductory explication could have revealed.

In the same way, you can show the businessman (in one short paragraph) typing desperately on his laptop in the doctor's waiting room, pleading on his mobile with his creditors until he's called in and, hearing the doctor's gentle life-sentence, suddenly, and for the first time, becoming absolutely still. His initial frenzy and his unaccustomed quiet will reveal more about how he got to that doctor's office than pages of introductory information. In addition, the narrative ball will already be rolling. We readers won't have to wait for the action to start: it's started!

What is that decision, what is that sudden alteration of circumstance that changes everything? What is that first domino? Tell yourself what your story is about: "It's about a young woman trapped in a small town who escapes to become a famous actress." Your first active verb is "escapes." That gives you your opening scene. She escapes. Or your story line could be: "A businessman at the end of his tether learns he has cancer and becomes a seeker after spiritual truth." The first active verb is "learns." That's where your story starts, in the doctor's office. Or "A wild young man, rebelling against being tamed, lights out for adventure." The active verb is "lights out," and that's what Huckleberry Finn does, to his own and literature's glory.

Cut to the action, but don't be tempted to start the book with a showy bang unless that showy bang is the initial action from which all other action flows. If you open with an epic space battle and then have to spend pages telling us how everybody got there, your flashback will bring your narrative to a protracted halt. The key words are: "from which all other action flows." The first scene is the first domino. The second domino has to be right behind it. That inexorably tumbling line is your story, action begetting action until the conclusion.

Your job, on page one, is to open the narrative window at the exact moment of the first tumble. This doesn't have to be in the very first line, but it does have to be in the very first scene. If your first thousand words don't contain the initial action, rewrite until they do. That's where your story begins. That's where to start.

Hook, Line, or Sinker

by Joy V. Formy-Duval

riting is much like fishing. Both require preparation, skill, and an abundance of patience. You flip the lid on that tackle box, look over your array of lures, and hope the one you choose will be irresistible. The right bait will hook that sucker before he knows what hit him. But on a bad day, that pretty thing dancing near the top of the water only teases him, and he teases you right back. And on a very bad day, that old fish will take one look at what you're offering and reject it outright, leaving you to wonder what the heck went wrong.

Now that the fishing is out of the way, let's get down to some serious business, focus our concentration on the objective, and get to work. First, go back and reread that first sentence you wrote several minutes ago. If you didn't know everything there was to know about this story your writing, would the beginning line grab you in the gut, tease you a bit, or fail to evoke the slightest emotion? Put both hands on your head and repeat after me: "Within the sphere of my hands lies raw creativity and the determination to mold a viable force capable of piercing that wall of unknowns." Of course, if anyone catches you holding your head, your eyes focused on a blank wall, your lips moving in a silent chant, don't bother explaining. People who don't write think we writers are a few french fries short of a happy meal anyway.

There is more to writing than merely telling your story. While the story line may be unique and appealing, how you present it determines whether your book is a bestseller, a moderate success, or an utter failure.

Writers don't always write sequentially. They may write the most exciting chapters first, or may even write the ending first. But, if writers expect that novel to find a good home, at some point they must write the real beginning. Somewhere in all those words is the perfect first sentence, that opening line that captivates the reader. When you start with the real beginning, readers can't tear themselves away from the scenes you've lived with, sweated over, and finally bled onto the page.

Sometimes when we pause to read our work aloud, we discover that the beginning we used wasn't the best beginning for the story. No action took place, no dynamic dialogue, nothing to inspire a reader to continue on the trip we've so carefully planned. While our original words may be important, we must come up with a scene that will draw the reader in, tease the imagination with speculation, convince him immediately to read the rest of the story.

> "Are you ready to die?"
> Karen Robards, *Heart Breaker*

First lines are like first impressions. You never get a second chance. A first line should provoke one or more of the senses. Do the words make bile rise in the throat? Do they squeeze the heart until tears roll down the cheeks? Do they conjure up the scent of cinnamon rolls baking and fond childhood memories? Do they make the reader hear that wind chime and feel that soft breeze? Can the mind's eye see the picture you have painted?

> On Sunday, something washed up on the shore.
> Susan Wiggs, *The Lightkeeper*

Susan Wiggs knows how to write a good first line. Had the narrator been expecting something to surface? Had he played a role in its submersion and perhaps hoped against hope that whatever floated to the top of the water would take weeks instead of days? How long had he waited, sweated, dreaded that inevitable day of reckoning?

Dexter Whitlaw carefully sealed the box, securing every seam
with a roll of masking tape he had stolen from Walmart the
day before. Linda Howard, *Kill & Tell*

Who is Dexter Whitlaw, what's in that box, and why would anyone
steal a fifty-nine-cent roll of masking tape?

I wasn't thinking about the man who'd blown himself up.
Kathy Reichs, *Deja Dead*

Who is the speaker, and what is he/she seeing to make the man who'd
just blown himself to smithereens so insignificant?

Cam called in markers, pulled strings, begged favors and
threw money in a dozen directions.
Nora Roberts, *Sea Swept*

Right from the start, we know Cam is a wheeler/dealer who doesn't live
by the same set of rules that most of us do. What is the driving force behind
such a man?

He hated his curly red hair and freckles.
Mary Lynn Baxter, *Lone Star Heat*

Baxter introduces her main characters immediately in the prologue. And
in Chapter 1, which begins eleven years later, "She looked down into a
bloody palm." Has this character stumbled onto a murder, or is she the
murderer? And what relationship does she have to the fellow who hates
how he looks?

Of all the writers I've surveyed, mystery novelist Lisa Gardner says
it best in *The Perfect Husband*. The introduction page begins, "Jim had
no hair on his head, not on his body." The prologue reads, "The first
time he saw her, he simply knew." And Chapter 1 begins, "J. T. Dillon
was drunk." Gardner is a skillful user of hooks, much to this reader's
delight.

All writers are readers, and while I read for pleasure, my subconscious picks up on the various voices of other writers, their opening lines, the effectiveness of the dialogue they use. So, as I said at the beginning of this article, go back and read your opening line as if you were a reader seeing it for the very first time. What kind of impression did you get? Are your fingers itching to turn the page, read more? Or is it so nondescript you wonder why in the world you put it there? Remember, you've worked hard to get that story on paper, and it deserves every chance to succeed in a competitive field where publishers, editors, and agents see more poorly written work than good. Hook them with that first line, and reel them in.

Robards, Karen. *Heartbreaker*. Dell, 1998 (paper), ISBN: 044021596X

Wiggs, Susan. *The Lightkeeper*. Mira Books, 2002 (paper), ISBN: 1551668807

Howard, Linda. *Kill & Tell*. Pocket Books, 1998 (paper), ISBN: 0671568833

Reichs, Kathy. *Deja Dead*. Pocket Books, 1997 (paper), ISBN: 0671011367

Roberts, Nora. *Sea Swept*. Jove Pubns, 2001 (paper), ISBN: 0515121843

Baxter, Mary Lynn. *Lone Star Heat*. Harlequin, 1997 (paper), ASIN: 1551662892

Gardner, Lisa. *The Perfect Husband*. Bantam Books, 1998 (reissue), ISBN: 0553576801

What's In A Name?

By Elizabeth Delisi

"What's in a name? that which we call a rose, By any other name would smell as sweet..." When Juliet spoke those words in the famous balcony scene of Shakespeare's *Romeo and Juliet*, she meant that Romeo would still be Romeo even if his last name weren't Montague, which made him an enemy of Juliet's family.

Alas, the same doesn't hold quite true for a novel. Its title shouldn't be regarded as unimportant and tacked on as an afterthought. While the story is the substance, the title is the first thing a reader sees. It identifies your story and begins its introduction to the reader. If the title is weak, readers may pass your book by without even sampling its prose. On the other hand, an effective title will grab the reader's attention and at least start him reading your work.

A good title does three things:

— It draws the reader's attention to your book

— It signals, to some extent, what to expect from the book

— It induces the reader to read a little farther.

Titles come in many varieties. They can be straightforward *(The Hunt for Red October*, by Tom Clancy; or *The Martian Chronicles*, by Ray Bradbury), or indirect, suggestive or veiled (*Cat's Eye*, by Margaret Atwood; or *Shadow of the Moon*, by M. M. Kaye). Some titles are esoteric, designed to pique a reader's curiosity while relying on a subtitle to focus the subject (*Fantastic Voyage II: Destination, Brain*, by Isaac Asimov; or *The Mummy; or, Ramses the Damned*, by Anne Rice). Some authors like to use word games in their titles (*Telltale Tics and Tremors*, by Harlan Ellison—words with the same initial sound; *The Accidental Tourist*, by Anne Tyler–juxtaposition of words with opposite meanings), while other titles seem familiar and are based on common phrases or themes (*It Came From Schenectady*, by Barry B. Longyear; or *Who's Afraid of Beowulf?* by Tom Holt).

How to come up with a title? One way is to start with a word designed to catch a reader's interest. Choose a word that's compelling–"murder," "darkness," "passion," "prisoner." Then take that word and play with it. For instance, if your word is "darkness," try adding adjectives: The Cold Darkness, The Waiting Darkness, The Crying Darkness. Or perhaps try a prepositional phrase: Darkness on My Mind, Darkness in the Nursery, Darkness in Daylight. Add a verb to the word: Darkness Follows, Darkness Watches, Darkness Speaks. You can add another noun: Darkness and Murder, Laughter and Darkness. Or try coupling the key word with an opposite word or concept: The Glaring Darkness, The Revealing Darkness, The Welcoming Darkness. One of these ideas may be just right.

A thesaurus and dictionary of famous quotations can be helpful. Write down several words that figure importantly in your story. Look up the words in the thesaurus to see whether any of the synonyms catch your fancy. Or take those same words and look them up in a dictionary of quotations; one of the quotes, when shaped to suit your purpose, may provide you with a title.

In some cases, a title will come to you before the story does. If you get an idea for an intriguing title, write it down. Once it has percolated in your subconscious for a while, a story may come to you that's tailor-made for that title. When you need an idea for a story and don't have one, fooling around with title ideas can give your imagination the jolt it needs.

There is no "proper" time to create your title. Some writers prefer not to put a title on a manuscript until the work is complete, while others come up with the title first, to give the story shape and focus.

Playing with a title can be a wonderful way to get over that "middle of the novel" slump and to get your creativity jump-started again. But whenever you come up with your title—first, midway, or last—make sure it's not least!

Some of the ideas in this article are adapted from: *How to Write Bestselling Fiction,* by Dean R. Koontz (Writer's Digest Books, Cincinnati, OH, 1981).

Readers love to be surprised, but only if you have
planted clues to support the ending.

Linear Versus Circular: The Means to an End

by Victoria Benson

Have you ever read a book that held your interest as you raced to find out how the hero would handle his crisis, only to be sorely disappointed by the ending? Chances are you haven't read another book by that author.

How do you, as writers, ensure that when your readers finish your book they are satisfied and eager to read more? The answer lies at the beginning of your project. You prepare by first deciding your ending, and follow by structuring your story toward that ending.

Will you follow a linear path to the climax and then end immediately after the conflict is resolved? Or will you bring the main character back to where he started, only with greater self-knowledge?

When the story ends after your protagonist struggles with a constant uphill battle toward the long, suspenseful climax and comes to a point of decision in order to solve the problem, you have employed the linear ending. Mysteries, suspense and action thrillers fall into this category.

Readers of best-selling novels by modern writers such as Tom Clancy and Michael Crichton don't want to spend time after the crisis reading additional chapters that show how the main character's life has changed because of his or her wonderful solution.

That is not to say the main character in a linear story doesn't ever change. At the point where he must decide on his direction in order to resolve the major conflict, he may change or he may remain steadfast on his pre-determined course. Often, the hero experiences an epiphany—a sudden understanding. This insight reveals some aspect of himself or the situation requiring his attention. In a mystery, he will suddenly figure out who committed the crime, or how it was done. In a more introspective work, the hero might see something about himself that needs to be addressed and changed.

Whether or not the protagonist changes, the way he solves the problem facing him must be supported by his actions up to that point. That leads us to surprise, or twist endings, commonplace in linear stories.

Readers love to be surprised, but only if you have planted clues to support the ending. You must carefully seed your story with actions, thoughts and dialogue that show consistency in your hero. But don't reveal ahead of time the answer to your mystery or the direction your main character will take at his crisis point. Your reader wants to guess, maybe even successfully figure out the puzzle, but he doesn't want you to underestimate his intelligence.

In the *Perry Mason* television series from the 1960s, Mason appeared to pull a rabbit from the hat at the end of each show when he disclosed the real murderer. But if you watched closely, he dropped hints beforehand to lead you toward his conclusion.

Circular endings, on the other hand, take the main character on a complex adventure that brings him back to the original point of departure. The crisis occurs not at the end, but earlier in the story. Let's look at this in more detail.

The hero faces a truth about himself at the climax, the point of conscious decision. This new knowledge can arrive as an epiphany or as the culmination of several events or circumstances that cause self-revelation. He then chooses his direction in solving the crisis. The course of action that follows, based upon his new understanding, provides the denouement, or the final resolution of the subplots. He then touches, in an actual or parallel way, the place where he began, now as a changed person.

For example, in *The Wizard Of Oz*, Dorothy leaves Kansas thinking as a child. She experiences an epiphany in Oz, then she returns to Kansas with a mature appreciation for her home and her life. In Dickens's *A Christmas Carol*, Scrooge recognizes his own greedy nature after the visitations of three ghosts. If the story ended there, the reader would be left not knowing how Scrooge would respond to his insightful revelation. Would he commit suicide, thinking he was an unredeemable soul? Or would he correct his wrong doings? Indeed, Dickens brings the story full circle to a happy Christmas celebration with Tiny Tim, reflecting Scrooge's growth.

The classic, *Gone With The Wind*, presents a circular ending with a longer denouement and more subplots for the heroine to resolve. The true climax, the turning point of the book, happens mid-way through the story, when Tara is all but destroyed. Scarlett vows to work the land herself and never to be hungry again. From that day on, all her decisions are filtered through that resolve. Tara comes first, even if it means she loses everyone dear to her. Her story begins and ends with Tara.

Readers respond favorably to revelation and growth in your main characters. One of the most difficult tasks in crafting a story is setting up your main character to reach the point of conscious decision—the point where he must choose to change in order to face the next phase of his life. This is when he finds the inner strength to succeed at something he failed at in the beginning, or he is able to stop doing something destructive.

The larger and grander the revelation and resolution, the greater the impact you will have on your reader. Who will forget Scarlett after Atlanta burns, standing on dry earth with a carrot in her fist? Or Rocky, facing almost certain defeat, determined to fight his opponent and win?

As writers, we have the responsibility to include our readers in the development and decision-making process of our main character. The protagonist must react with consistency and logic in order for us to believe his final course of action. Use thoughts, speech and actions to pepper your story with hints pointing to your hero's eventual decision, so his solution of choice is not out of character.

How disappointing would you find the ending of *Braveheart* if Wallace had bravely battled for love, revenge and freedom, only to fall apart and beg the executioner for mercy, then slink off into obscurity? Granted, *Braveheart* has a sad ending, but Wallace's moral principals triumph above all.

Wallace also exemplifies the hero who experiences a self-revelation and a personal victory, but finds the ultimate foe to be unbeatable, such as the person facing his own death or that of a loved one.

You also need to decide whether your protagonist lives or dies at the end of your story. People generally prefer the ending in which the main character successfully faces his true nature and defeats the flaw or element that threatens to destroy him. Both Scrooge and Rocky exemplify this type of hero.

During the Depression era of American literature, slice-of-life stories utilized endings in which the self-revelation destroys the hero. *Death Of A Salesman*'s Willy Lowman can't live believing he failed to provide for his family. Although the ending is sad, Lowman's choice of direction at the climax is in character, as shown by Miller's skillful development throughout the story.

In all cases, endings must leave your story on a level higher or lower than where it began. To accomplish this successfully, you must decide before you start writing whether your hero will fail or succeed, change or remain steadfast, and whether his journey will end with the climax or proceed with additional introspection.

Once you know the style of your ending, you will know how to develop your main characters from the beginning in a supportive, consistent manner. When you have successfully completed this task, your readers will close your book and nod, saying, "Yes, that was the way this story had to end."

Baum, L. Frank. *The Wizard Of Oz.* Troll Assoc., 1985 (reprint) ASIN: 0816704678

Dickens, Charles. *A Christmas Carol.* Trafalgar Square, 2001 (reprint), ISBN: 186205130

Mitchell, Margaret. *Gone With The Wind.* Scribner, 1996 (reprint), ISBN: 068483068X

Miller, Arthur. *Death Of A Salesman.* Viking Penguin, 1998, ISBN: 0141180978

Structure, Style And Voice

Scenes that Write Themselves

by Wendy Walton Dickerman

How many times have you imagined a specific scenario for your novel when suddenly, without warning, your script begins writing itself differently? When was the last time you were typing along, getting ready to have that brilliant, handsome, sexually maniacal judge kill your snoopy, borderline kooky/kinky newspaper reporter—but, as you begin to set the scene, your heart racing as you go for the kill, suddenly something alters? Your fingers are typing along, but, amazingly, the story twists, turns, bends inside out, and you find that the evil maniac has (gasp!) fallen for the sexy snoop, and, even more shocking, she is enthralled with him. Gotcha! Your novel now has a mind of its own, ready to override your carefully thought-out plans.

What do you do when this happens? Do you fiercely resist the changes, insisting on your predetermined path, or do you let the story have free reign to see what happens, which might benefit the plot? I'd opt for the latter, flowing with the scene as it unfolds, looking to see whether or not the changes enhance the story or dash it upon the rocky shoals. When a story strays, does this mean that some part of your psyche has been plotting the change all along? Or is this a ruse to mess up the carefully wrought storyline and lead you to disaster?

If the result keeps the story humming along, your creative juices flowing, and your mind saying "Yes, yes, yes," then you probably have a genie in your bottle, and should be grateful. If, however, the alteration makes you befuddled and strangles your forward motion, you should rethink the scene, perhaps returning to the original plan, or melding the two possibilities into a more propitious direction.

Was it perhaps too hard to murder your sexy snoop? Had you grown too fond of her? Was her loss going to be more than you could bear? Were you trying to soften and subtly humanize your maniacal murderer? What could explain your motives for such a change? Were you trying to sabotage the story, undermine the successful completion of a novel you weren't certain you wanted even to be associated with? Or was the plot alteration a cunning change of pace, a quirky, surprising curve, complicating and moving the plot into virgin territory, giving you rich fodder for the story?

How can you know which it is? The answer is...you can't. You have to trust your instincts to let go and write what *wants* to be written. Then you have to trust your insight and judgment about whether to keep it or scrub the scene's mission. Have no doubt that it will fight for its survival, craftily convincing you of its righteous place in history, but you'll have to believe your gut response to the changes as they fit with the whole. Maybe you'll scrub the entire novel, maybe only that one scene. Perchance you'll trade your villain for a spartan monk, living amidst the sinners of a big city. Maybe you'll stop having that second glass of wine before you start writing. Maybe you'll just take a nap, and when you wake, the novel will sit beside you, completely finished, gleaming in the moonlight as the stars go nova, just as your publisher calls to congratulate you on winning the Pulitzer.

Who can say?

Strengthen Your Writing With Narrative Arcs

by John Moir

Narrative arcs—the intentional repetition of words and events in a novel—add power and emotional resonance to your writing. As a chorus does a song, narrative connections give your story line cohesion and power.

I first learned of narrative arcs when I heard the award-winning young-adult author Paul Fleischman speak at a writer's conference about the similarities between writing and music. He talked about how a piece of writing is like a symphony—there is a main theme, then variations on this theme, and then perhaps some minor themes. He showed how repeating these themes at strategic places is very powerful and noted that writing, like music, gains strength from these arcs of repetition.

Fleischman uses these arcs in his novel *The Borning Room,* which recounts the life of frontier-woman Georgina Lott. The story takes place more than a century ago, when houses often had small "borning rooms" set aside for birth, illness, and death. The novel opens with the story of Georgina's difficult birth. Many details of this scene—a maple tree outside the window, the hooting of owls, the German midwife—appear again, woven into a much later section of the novel, when Georgina gives birth to her own daughter. The repetition of these details links the two scenes and makes each more powerful.

Narrative arcs can be formed in two ways. The first is the repetition of an event or situation that gathers meaning when it is repeated. The second is the repetition of certain words, phrases, or even names.

Ken Follett combined both techniques in his epic novel of the Middle Ages, *The Pillars of the Earth*. The book begins with a young man about to be hung for a crime he did not commit. The opening line of the book reads "The small boys came early to the hanging."

Although the novel stretches over several decades and is more than nine hundred pages long, Follett ends the story just as it started: We are at the same gallows, it is dawn, and there is to be another hanging. With a wonderful sense of justice fulfilled, we read that this time the man to be hung is the villain responsible for falsely accusing the youth so many years before. The narrative arc gives us a satisfying sense of completion.

But Follett takes this technique one step further. The final hanging scene opens with the same line as the book's first chapter: "The small boys came early to the hanging."

These words and story line, arcing back to the opening of the book, form an emotional and structural bridge for the novel. But not every repetition need be so dramatic. Even small narrative arcs can be effective in helping the flow of your story. Just as the gun on the wall must be used before the last act of a play, first mentioning something peripherally gives the reader a sense of recognition when it later moves center stage.

Nonfiction can also make use of arcs. Three quarters of the way through Sylvia Boorstein's bestselling book on Buddhism, *It's Easier Than You Think*, she tells the tale of a friend who is dying. The friend talks about what is important in life and how even simple things can carry great meaning. She mentions one of her favorite recipes, telling how happy it makes people, and asks that it be shared at her memorial service.

The last page of Boorstein's book is a simple rendering of that special recipe. It provides a narrative arc that packs an emotional wallop for readers as they recall the words and thoughts of her dying friend.

Sometimes narrative arcs happen by happy accident in our stories. But good writers rely on more than narrative luck. Once a story is roughed out, finding ways to link back and forth and so tie your story together gives it power and cohesiveness.

Finally, if you want a crash course in using narrative arcs, check out the video of the movie *Avalon*. Not only is it a wonderful film, but the underpinnings of the story are based on this powerful storytelling technique.

Fleischman, Paul. *The Borning Room*. HarperTrophy, 1993 (reprint), ISBN: 0064470997

Follett, Ken. *The Pillars of the Earth*, Signet. 1996 (reissue) ISBN: 0451166892

Boorstein, Sylvia. *It's Easier Than You Think: The Buddhist Way to Happiness*. Harper San Francisco, 1997, ISBN: 0062512943

Using Mood In Novel Writing

by Gwen Y. Fortune

Today I am looking through the window beside my computer. Outside, at close range, perhaps twelve feet, I see the rough bark of a pine tree about twelve inches in diameter. The texture of this bark captures my attention: variations of medium to light brown that have a faint pink cast as the sunlight strikes the bark in several places. The light changes just a bit as the branch of a cypress tree moves with the wind, creating a wash across one side of the tree. This is a very young branch, and it bends easily. Farther away, twenty-five or thirty feet, limbs are stationary. The wind is selective.

One hundred feet further, I glimpse an expanse of sunny green lawn. My neighbor mows his grass.

The physical surroundings in just a small viewing area can have a profound effect on the words I write today. I can and perhaps will write a happy scene in the novel in process. The mood evoked by the sun, the temperature and the quiet—it is a holiday, and no one is stirring—suggests a love scene, or one where the woods shelter something unknown but not sinister. I didn't hear cars moving on the lane at the usual 6:00 AM this morning. A peacefulness, an easy energy, is in the air.

Yesterday, the sky was overcast all day. I closed the windows that had been open to the warmth of late spring, even thought of turning the thermostat back to "heat." Instead, I sat in bed and covered my shoulders with an afghan while I read. As I contemplated the day, it was obvious that anything I wrote would be melancholy. There would be a sinister event emerging from the woods. Only a mighty tug could have pulled me from my lethargy—given my mood, nothing happy would evolve from my fingers on the keyboard.

What do writers do to "work with" their personal energy states, or moods? Some writers say they are able to enter a state of detachment. But why not use moods consciously? Whether we are story writers, novelists, or poets, my suggestion is to acknowledge, investigate, and embrace the mood evoked by circumstance, and then use it. Modification is always possible. I think that going with the energy already generated can be more productive, creatively and practically.

We are, despite arguments or desires to the contrary, bone, body, and blood, with intricate brain and emotional functions at play both awake and asleep. Considering contrasting moods, as in my examples of yesterday and today, and being aware of the effects of physical and emotional environments can help a writer produce better writing. A variety of scenes, characterizations, and descriptions can emerge from the immediacy and effect of a writer's moods. If we write and file the results, accessing them as our writing needs suggest, we can think of the *mood* work as research. Remember all the 3" x 5" file cards we once used for a college paper, the conclusion representing only a fraction of the stacks of cardboard we used? I think that writing from mood can produce far less unused "product" than did all the time and energy expended in those earlier days.

I look up from the keyboard—after half an hour of working on a first draft—and see that the first tree outside my window looks different. The bark is more uniform; the sun has moved further west. The wind is absolutely calm so that the shadows of pink and brown are stationary for a while. On the other side of my property line, my neighbor's open, sunny yard seems the same—but if I go outside, I'm sure I will see something different. Ah, the wind has just moved the leaves of several trees that are growing rapidly following the devastation of Hurricane Fran a few years ago. Now, that brings on another mood.

If You've Heard It Once...

by Ann M. Beardsley

You've heard it a thousand times: "Show, don't tell." But how often do those articles exhorting you to do that proceed to tell you just how to show? The following suggestions are meant to help you make your writing as concrete and as specific as possible.

1) *Use details*, not generic descriptions. Is he smoking a cigarette or a Marlboro? The latter brings up images of the Marlboro Man, ten-gallon hat and all. A cigarette could suggest anything from a slimeball on the make to an elegant diner in a smoking jacket. As readers, we get no clues from just plain "cigarette." Make every word work for you.

2) *Avoid lists.* "He was a tall man, with magnetic dark eyes, a shock of hair that fell rakishly over one eye, and a lopsided grin betokening a sense of humor." Compare that description with this one: "Her eyes locked on his, unable to escape their magnetism until he smiled. His lopsided grin hinted at a sense of humor, as did the shock of dark hair failing rakishly over his right eye." Okay, tall, dark, and handsome may not be your cup of tea, but lists belong in the grocery. Keep your reader engaged.

3) *Watch out for those weak verbs*: "was," "is," "be," "are," and "were." Use strong one-part verbs: "Jack strode down the street, his Western books clicking on the pavement," not "Jack was walking down the street wearing his Western boots."

4) *Avoid prosaic descriptions* whenever possible. "She was a beautiful woman." Try using someone's reaction to her instead. "Kelly felt a jolt of envy as she looked at the other woman." "Men's heads turned when Alice walked down the street, even when she wore old blue jeans and a baggy sweatshirt."

5) *Get rid of most of your adverbs*. Instead of "She ran quickly, easily outdistancing the two men following her." Try "She broke into a sweat, half a block after the two men following her had given up in a torrent of curses and heavy breathing."

6) *Choose at random a section* from your own writing, perhaps a paragraph or a short scene. Ask yourself what you want the reader to get out of that paragraph. Action? Setting? A sense of character? A clue you've hidden there? Then use the powerful verbs and select adjectives to accomplish that purpose. Are you trying to evoke a sense of horror? Find dark, forbidding words that describe the elements you want to emphasize. Don't describe the leafless tree unless this description can be used to increase the tension.

7) And last, *try listening to radio stories* (not books on tape) such as "Moon over Morocco" or "Ruby, the Galactic Gumshoe." With virtually no description, they manage through dialogue to get the reader involved without ever telling what color hair the hero has, what the heroine looks like, and what she did for the first thirty-five or so years of her life. Details can be nice, but they should have a direct bearing on your story.

As with a house of cards that collapses when the bottom card is pulled out, so the resolution of one major conflict leads inevitably to the resolution of all.

You Can Write A Novel—Or A Symphony

by Elizabeth Delisi

"Music resembles poetry; in each / Are nameless graces which no methods teach, / And which a master-hand alone can reach."

So says Alexander Pope in *An Essay on Criticism*. It may be true that an inborn, indefinable spark of creativity is helpful, or even necessary, in generating a work of art. But there is much in music and in literature that can be defined; there is a characteristic structure under the surface that can be analyzed and learned from. The Italian novelist Alberto Moravia understood the similar structures of music and literature: "I view the novel, a single novel as well as a writer's entire corpus, as a musical composition in which the characters are themes, from variation to variation completing an entire parabola; similarly for the themes themselves." [Quoted in *Writers on Writing* by Jon Winokur]

Let's look at the makeup of both music and literature, and see how they are alike.

"Sonata form" is the structure upon which many types of musical compositions are based. It is used as the backbone for single movements in the sonata, the concert overture, the concerto, and the symphony.

Sonata form typically begins with a brief introduction, then moves quickly into the theme, or exposition. Usually more than one theme is presented, and a strong conflict is set up between the first and second themes, or between the principal and alternate keys.

After the presentation of major themes comes the development section. Themes are expanded, fragmented, inverted, changed from one key to another or from major to minor. Short musical ideas, or motives, are developed and may take on unexpected emotional overtones. According to Roger Kamien in *Music: An Appreciation*, "The development is often the most dramatic section of the movement. The listener may be kept off balance as the music moves restlessly through several different keys. Through these rapid modulations, the harmonic tension is heightened."

The tension builds to such an extent that a resolution is necessary. During the recapitulation section, the themes are restated, but they have all resolved to the principal key. Tension ebbs away, leading to the coda section, which leaves the listener with a powerful sense of conclusion.

A similar structure underlies the novel. The book may begin with an introduction, taking the form of a prologue, but it swiftly moves to present the main characters and conflicts. As in sonata form, conflicts must immediately arise between these characters, and between the characters and their environment. Internal (emotional) and external (environmental) conflicts must both be present, setting up the basis for the development section of the novel.

During the development section, which encompasses the major part of the book, the themes and conflicts presented in the opening are expanded upon. As with music, the story takes unexpected twists and turns, producing tension and unforeseen consequences and thereby heightening the emotional intensity. As the novel progresses, the reader is drawn in by the ever-more-complex series of evolving, interrelated events.

The conflicts in your story should be layered, or sandwiched, one upon the other, until they're tied into a nearly inconvertible knot. The motivation of your characters is what leads to this sequence of struggles. The motivation for a character's internal conflicts may come from one or many sources: for example, childhood experiences; relationships with parents or siblings; early trauma; societal pressures; prejudice; attitudes towards sex, religion, or money; or prior love relationships. External conflicts should tie in closely with the character's inner struggles, heightening the tension even further.

Just when the reader can stand no more strain and demands a conclusion, the resolution or recapitulation takes place. Each important theme is brought back, but through the evolution of events in the novel and the growth of the characters, conflicts are now able to be resolved. As with a house of cards that collapses when the bottom card is pulled out, so the resolution of one major conflict leads inevitably to the resolution of all. At last everything dovetails, and the denouement allows the reader to close the book with a satisfied sigh.

So, the next time you sit down to plot out a new book, put your favorite symphony on the stereo—and take a lesson from the pros. As Arthur O'Shaughnessy said in his ode, *The Music-Makers*, "We are the music-makers, / And we are the dreamers of dreams."

Alexander Pope and Arthur O'Shaughnessy in *Dictionary of Quotations*, collected and arranged by Bergen Evans, Avenel Books, 1978, ISBN: 0517268094

Kamien, Roger. *Music: An Appreciation*, WCB/McGraw-Hill, 1999 (seventh edition), ISBN: 0072902000

Winokur, Jon. *Writers on Writing*, Running Press, 1990, ASIN: 0894718770

Who Needs Flashbacks

by Maria Considine

*F*lashbacks are peculiar devices—many people fight shy of them, but most writers have, at some time or other, felt the need to use them. The beginning writer is often told: "Start your story at the point of change." But the problem with this strategy is that the reader will not have relevant background information, and hence the writer will be tempted to step back from the story and fill in the gaps for a while. Not a bad idea, really. But if a flashback is to work the writer must be aware of the strengths and weaknesses of this device.

A story thrives on forward movement. This can be movement on the physical plane—e.g. a crime committed, clues deciphered, a murderer apprehended. Or it can be movement on the emotional plane—the hero faces a problem, works through the problem, and arrives at self-knowledge. In each case there has been a series of forward steps. But flashbacks disrupt this orderly progression and invite the reader to step back in time. For such a course of action to be effective, the flashback episode must have a high interest level and must serve a definite purpose. Before using this device a writer should consider its effectiveness—does this episode advance the plot, does it affect the emotional movement of the piece, does it flesh out the characters in any way, does it change the mood or direction of the story? If the flashback doesn't do any of these things, chances are that it is not needed, and the writer should convey the necessary information some other way.

If the writer decides to use a flashback, there are still other points to consider. The flashback is a part of the story, a detour in the movement of the plot. If it is too long the reader can get lost in its meandering, so it is best kept short. A flashback must maintain interest in the outcome of the story—if the reader is bored to death by the digression, he is not likely to want to come back into the mainstream of the story. So the interruption must be vividly written and should not burden the reader with excessive exposition. Details can always be supplied later.

A potential problem with flashbacks is the way the transition is made between the past incident and the present time in the story. Unless the connection is skillfully executed it can appear amateurish. We are all familiar with the kind of story that begins "I was rooting through a pile of old school photos when I came across a picture of my graduating class. At once I thought about Mary and I remembered..." The writer then launches into a blow-by-blow account of a teenage romance. This approach is awkward and obvious.

The flashback should be presented directly with as little preamble as possible and the return to the main story must happen unobtrusively. If a cue is needed to signal the return to the present, try leaving a few blank lines rather then using a hackneyed phrase such as "...brought him back to the present. "

When handled with care, flashbacks can be gracefully informative. And because they slow down the action, they can help with a story's pacing. Like the intermittent bits of level ground you sometimes come across on an arduous hill climb, they give a bit of breathing space and lower the tension for a while. With practice, a writer can learn to use flashbacks for maximum dramatic effect, heightening the reader's pleasure in a story's ebb and flow.

On Structuring A Novel

by Eileen Alcorn Workman

S o often these days, when we finish reading a book, our initial reaction is a sense of disappointment. Sure, the prose sang, the metaphors crackled and the characters were unusual enough, but somewhere along the way we seemed to lose interest in what was happening. Why, you might ask, does this occur? The answer, in short, is that when it comes to novels, neither talent nor clever prose are enough to capture and keep the attention of a modern-day reader. What today's readers want and what editors buy are stories, strong ones, with beginnings, middles, and endings that hang together. Stories that weave a tale, stories that transport a reader to faraway places on the wings of his or her imagination, stories that create a lasting emotional impact on a reader.

How, then, does a writer go about creating such a story? The easiest way is to follow the trail blazed by the ancient Greeks as they wrote the earliest surviving stage plays—the three-act method. Now, granted, this simple way isn't necessarily the best or only method for structuring a story—all I'm suggesting is that it's a traditional method that has proven itself to be successful for many years.

Before we evaluate the three act method, however, let's look at the basic elements that comprise a classic story. One hallmark of the classical method of storytelling is the closed ending, whereby all the important questions raised by the story are answered. In addition, the classic story's timeline will flow continuously, unlike, say, that of a story such as *Pulp Fiction*, where time jumps and skitters all over the place. A third requirement is that the story be stable; once established, the rules of the story mustn't change. A city may not suddenly spring up on some distant planet unless the writer has established from the start that his is a science-fiction story; a dead person should not return to life unless the plot contains a mystery that makes such a plot twist believable.

Fourth, the events in a classic story must unfold in a cause-and-effect progression rather than happen on the basis of sheer coincidence. The classic story structure depends on the concept of change. An event must occur within the story that changes the protagonist profoundly. And, speaking of protagonists, classic structure dictates that there be but one (okay, maybe two) and that he or she be active in addressing the story's root problem. In other words, the cause affects the protagonist directly, effecting a profound internal change.

How best, you might be wondering, to format such a classic story? In the first act of a classic play, the *inciting incident* occurs. In other words, something happens to upset the natural balance of the protagonist's world. Act 1, therefore, has a very big job to do. It must set the big-picture scene for the reader and determine the nature (genre) of the story, as well as establish the primary character and propel the reader headlong into the protagonist's main problem. A lot to ask from the first 75-100 pages of a novel, you say? Not really. A screenplay accomplishes all this work in the first 15-20 pages; a short story, typically, in the first few paragraphs.

Where act 1 closes, act 2 picks up the pace by creating progressively tougher complications for our protagonist. If we thought what happened to our hero in act one was bad, just wait until we see what happens next! Spiraling problems are met with more desperate attempts by our protagonist to extricate himself from trouble, which only—naturally—lead to even bigger problems for our hero. By the climactic end of act 2—the big bang, if you will—the reader should be a) convinced the protagonist has finally met his doom (if this is a comedy or happy story), or b) convinced the protagonist has found the key to happiness (if this is a tragic story). Because of its increasing complexity, act 2 will typically be two or three times the length of the more pithy introductory Act One.

Act 3, in a nutshell, reveals the ultimate story reversal to the reader. Just at the point where the reader is convinced things are finally going as badly (in a comedy) or as wonderfully (in a tragedy) as possible under the circumstances (the end of act 2), the writer pulls the rug out from under his feet. Think *of Romeo And Juliet*; act 2 ends with Juliet hurrying off to Friar Lawrence's cell to marry Romeo. A happy ending? We wish. But Shakespeare's classic act 3 of this tragedy serves up the cruelest twist of all—the death of the star-crossed lovers into whose fates we've invested such energy and emotion.

In a happily-ending classic tale such as Emily Bronte's *Jane Eyre*, act 2 ends with Jane's fleeing Thornfeld Hall after learning of her beloved Mr. Rochester's unfortunate marriage to another, with her vowing never to see him again. The reader is convinced Jane will never find happiness with Mr. Rochester, at least until act 3 transports her back into his waiting and loving arms.

And there you have it. That's all there is to writing a three-act novel; it's that simple. So easy that, at this point, you may find yourself questioning the usefulness of the process, wondering if maybe it's too simple, too formulaic, too *tried* to be *true*? If so, let me suggest you take a few minutes to review mentally the most recent blockbuster films and best-selling works of mainstream fiction you've read or seen. Make the attempt at breaking them down act by act, and I think you'll find most—if not all—follow this very classic, very successful structure. Why? Because it's the way great stories have been told for thousands of years.

Plotting/Outlines

The Ten Commandments For Successful Plotting

by Eileen Alcorn Workman

1. Thou shalt know thine ending before thou beginnest thy beginning.

Seems simple, right? Yet too often I've heard would-be writers state that it's far more fun to be "surprised" by their own story outcomes. Unfortunately for them, good writing—satisfying though it is—is hard work. If you want to have fun, go to Disneyland. Good writing requires the author to foreshadow, to create red herrings, to form a trail of words that the reader (in hindsight) will realize led to the strongest possible outcome for that story. These feats are nearly impossible unless you, as writer, know exactly where your story idea is heading while you write.

2. Thou shalt not cheat thy reader by leaving out critical details.

Have you ever read a novel where, at the end, the writer divulges that the heroine has cleverly traced the serial number of the gun she'd found at the crime scene back to the murderer? The only problem is, the reader never learned about the gun—a capital plotting sin. Bad writers (and lazy ones) try to "get away" with this kind of trickery all the time. It's a consequence of that desire to "surprise" the reader, to conceal things until the last possible moment. But the truth is that tricky endings like this one don't surprise the reader—they merely make him crazy. Don't withhold essential information. If you do, some enraged reader is likely to track you down and eat your firstborn child.

3. Thou shalt not allow thy characters to romp aimlessly through the garden of thy story.

Characters, like people, need purpose. Don't inject them into a scene unless they have a role to fulfill. And, whatever the purpose, make it relate in some meaningful way to your story. A reader doesn't need an entire scene replaying Harry's nervous breakdown from three years back unless Harry's mental history is crucial to explaining Harry's current state of mind, which in turn must be crucial to the story. If it's not, a single line of well-placed dialogue will provide the reader with a sense of who Harry is, with far less waste.

4. Thou shalt honor thy characters, for they are all God's children.

And who is God in a novel but you? By applying your imagination, you have birthed a group of individuals, each possessing a unique set of strengths, weaknesses, fears, hopes and dreams. Having set the stage and drawn the outline for your story, get out of the way. Allow your characters to realize their true natures. Do not force a character to act contrary to his or her nature merely to further your plot; doing so is the surest way to make your reader distrust you. If a disagreement arises between story and character, you must either change the plot or change the character. If something has to give, don't make it the reader.

5. Thou shalt make thy hero suffer at every turn.

Again, this seems to be common sense, but all too often we fall in love with our heros. Falling in love with a character is a good thing— the more passionate we feel about our hero, the more passionately we will write about his problems. The temptation, however, is to let our hero off the hook because we hate to see him in pain. Still, it is precisely that pain (and concern about how it will end) that keeps the reader turning the pages. Prolong the agony.

6. Thou shalt offer a message; furthermore, thou shalt know thy message and weave it into thy story.

The message you offer doesn't have to be anything deep or particularly spiritual. The best story messages are those that explore some theme or aspect of life that has relevance to the writer. Does the notion of unrequited love trigger your interest? Terrific! You can write literally dozens of stories centered on the concept of unrequited love. Explore it from more than one angle, both the comic and the tragic. Change the characters, change the setting, change the outcome. Play with the nuances of missed cues, third-party interference, social and religious constraints. Mold the message and make it uniquely yours, but have one. Your readers expect it.

7. Thou shalt not kill, unless killing is crucial for the furtherance of thy story. Neither shalt thou commit needless adultery, insert obligatory sex scenes, or in general create unnecessary distractions that detract from the truth of thy message.

Many writers believe that for a novel to sell in today's market, it must include at least one OSS (obligatory sex scene). This is patently untrue. Thousands of novels are published each year with nary a reference to sex. Nor do most New York editors require scenes of murder and mayhem to spice up a story. A strong, fresh plot and believable characters are the only must-haves. Remember, the greatest sex scenes in the world can't shore up a flagging plot or round out flat characterizations.

8. Thou shalt outline thy story, then edit thy outline until thy idea is fully realized.

I cannot overstress the importance of having a road map for your journey. Writing a novel without one is like baking a cake without a recipe, pans, or any standard ingredients. One out of a thousand cooks might be talented enough to pull it off—but most of us aren't that intuitive or lucky.

9. Thou shalt not allow the tension in thy story to dissipate.

As soon as the tension in a story dissipates, the reader has been given an incentive to put down the book. And the one thing we do not want to give our readers is an easy excuse to stop reading. Therefore, whenever a story issue is resolved, it behooves you to introduce a fresh complication immediately—preferably one that puts the hero at even greater risk than did the problem he has just overcome.

10. Thou shalt fulfill the covenant(s) thou makest with thy reader.

A novel, by its very nature, forges a covenant between the writer and the reader. When a reader picks up a book, he is agreeing to dedicate several irrecoverable hours of his life to discovering what it is the writer has to say. This means that you, as writer, have an obligation to say something interesting, preferably in a fresh and insightful way. Furthermore, if your title and first few paragraphs imply that your book will be a romance, then by all means make your story romantic. If you begin writing what seems to be a hard-boiled present-day mystery, do not move the story to the planet Gothrup and turn your hero into a beetle on page 57. Neither should you change your point-of-view style or voices midstream, nor change your hero and/or antagonist once your premise has been established.

The cardinal sin, the one most guaranteed to violate the covenant between reader and writer, is to lie. Nothing is more likely to cause a reader to toss a book against a wall than being dragged out of a fictive dream by a writer's deception. Therefore, truly dead people must stay dead unless your story permits otherwise by way of a ghostly opening. If a mysterious blond woman is described as committing the murders, the killer in the end must not be an unremarkable bald man. In short, good writers use magic, not trickery, to amaze and delight their readers.

Sequences are made up of scenes, and they deal with complications the character faces along the way.

Scenes and Chapters

by C. J. Hannah

When you make the shift from short story to novel, my advice is to over-prepare. I outlined my first novel, not only chapter by chapter, but scene by scene, before I ever wrote a word of prose. I knew from my short-story writing that I was good at creating settings, so I worked with settings to help generate a structure for the novel. Additionally, I knew the central character in my story and the conflict with which he was involved.

Then I did a very pedestrian but necessary thing. I decided to write a novel of exactly twenty chapters, with each chapter to be around 3500 words, the length of short stories I had written and had published, for a manuscript total of 70,000 words. However, the danger there was evident: I might end up with a string of short stories only casually connected. So, when I set up my outline, I also imposed a chronological limitation on it. The story had to take place within three days. Okay, twenty chapters, three days— and within those days, I decided, I wanted certain events to occur at certain times of day (dawn, early morning, dusk, etc.) for (dare I say it) symbolic reasons. Understand, all this detailed outlining was coming from my basic fear that, as a short-story writer, I didn't have enough to say for a novel.

Now I began to consider what should happen in each chapter. At this point, the scene versus chapter idea came to mind. My first ideas for chapters were too general, too ambitious, or too illustrative of that short-story tendency to be highly focused—to deal with conflict, complication, crisis, and conclusion all in 3500 words. No good for a novel.

That meant chapters had to be handled differently. My first inclination was to set up a series of complications that would test the central character in various ways as he progressed toward the climax. That was more promising, but scheduling one complication per chapter seemed ridiculous. And then I began to understand something about sequences and scenes.

Sequences are made up of scenes, and they deal with complications the character faces along the way. Some sequences are very short, maybe two scenes long, and usually relate to subplots or add depth to characterization. Other sequences are very long and include many scenes. These are usually directly related to the main conflict and are more significant. In order to understand the difference between sequence and scene, which before I had just *felt* more than anything else, I spent a week going to movies, from the best to the worst. I took along a clipboard, and I plotted sequences and scenes. I found that the best movies had about fifteen sequences. The worst had thirty or more. The fifteen-sequence movies used a lot of dialogue in very intense scenes and were clearly character driven, whereas the thirty-plus sequences were action driven. After a week of viewing, I knew what a sequence should be.

Once I began plotting out my sequences within the chapter and chronology structure I'd set myself, I discovered pace. Long sequences (the ones dealing with the most significant points covering several chapters) had to have something within them to keep the story moving, such as subplots, interesting minor characters, strong and unique settings, powerful dialogue, etc. Shorter sequences were usually action based, strong in dialogue and physical movement.

Once I began writing the novel, one major structural change emerged. At the outset of the story, there is a heavy use of memory, idyllic at the beginning, that contrasted with the horror of the present. Childhood memories dominate the first half of the novel, interrupted by brief passages of present-time reality, but at the half way point of the book, the present has equal time with the past because the protagonist has discovered something about his past in recalling it. From that point on, the past memories begin to recede in importance, and his present reality begins to dominate, until in the last two chapters he is totally in the present. He has come to terms with his childhood and is able to live in the present. The discovery I made here is that structure and theme can be interrelated beautifully and subtly.

One other point should be made about this kind of detailed outline: I put it on a large piece of cardboard and nailed it to the wall over my typewriter so that when I sat down each day, I knew exactly what I had to do. The outline defined my job. There were my tasks, listed for me.

I think it was after three chapters that I realized I could write a novel. In fact, a new problem emerged: how to stop at 70,000 words!

In The Beginning Was The End: The Purpose And Process Of Outlining

by Eileen Alcorn Workman

"If you don't know where you're going, any road will get you there." Such clichés survive, possibly because a nugget of truth exists behind the words.

True, there are no such things as "hard and fast" writing rules. It's also true that, occasionally, a writer is born who can sit down and craft the perfect novel without having the foggiest notion of where his story is headed. But for the rest, you who've tossed out countless pages of work because you've lost the story thread or sat frozen in front of your keyboard because you haven't a clue as to where to take your characters, learning how to outline can solve many of your problems. And it may make all the difference when it comes time to sell your work.

Writers create dozens of excuses as to why one shouldn't outline: it stifles creativity, prevents spontaneous character development, erodes the enthusiasm of the writer for the project, turns the art of writing into a methodical chore. The list is endless. The truth is, the reason most writers refuse to outline is simple: it's hard work. A child builds a Lego castle as an expression of creativity, but how many adults would venture to live inside it? Open-air roofs, non-existent doors and windows, and staircases leading to nowhere are all charming effects in the Lego world. But those same structural flaws would render a real house uninhabitable.

So it is with books. Go back and examine your favorite novels, and you'll find the best, most satisfying stories contain countless elements of foreshadowing. In hindsight, each story follows a path that leads to the one and only place where that tale could rightfully end, despite the occasional pleasant side trip. Why? Because the author planned it that way. Such strong story-writing isn't an accident or a blessing but the result of long hours, days, or weeks of careful consideration about what ought to be happening to the characters throughout the story.

Real life is full of randomness: part coincidence, part chance, part accident of birth. Fiction, however, is a different kind of experience. A novel is built around rising tension, the infliction of ever-increasing risk or misery upon the main character, strong pacing, and colorful dialogue. You need to know where your story is headed if you ever hope to coax your cast of characters (who will likely develop their own agendas along the way) to the finish line in the most exciting and least indulgent fashion. Thus, an outline starts, not with the beginning, but with "The End."

Ask yourself which characters will still be alive when your story closes; which have suffered, grown and changed, gotten older and wiser, or become bitter and frozen into place? Is it a happy ending or a tragedy? Make notes (copious ones) containing the relevant facts about your characters, their motivations, and their disappointments and achievements. Now you're ready to begin unraveling your story from the end to the beginning. (If it helps, refer to a timeline or calendar to help you chronicle the story's main events.) Use index cards for this part. On each card, record one important scene, climactic event, new problem, or character clash you've envisioned. Once you've jotted down all of your ideas, no matter how crazy they seem, place your notecards on the floor and try putting them into sequence. Then read through the sequenced cards. (If using cards drives you nuts, use a word-processing program instead. The "delete" and "move" keys work almost as well.)

Does your story flow succinctly from start to finish? Or does your notecard lineup reveal holes, sagging story areas, scenic roads to nowhere, or big chunks of action or time in which your major characters vanish? Is your decision to have your hero travel to Buenos Aires a strong one or just the first thing that came to your head? What if he went to Cuba or Maui instead? Would it strengthen or weaken your story? If his wife leaves him in scene seven, does your hero reconcile with her in scene nine or fifty-nine? Which works better, or does the couple need to reconcile at all? Do you have too few characters or too many to track? Did you introduce a unique or important detail in scene 12 and forget to work it back into the story line later? Are your characters' actions and motivations consistent with their personal development, or did you make a weak, boring choice for expediency's sake? Is your hero's level of risk or personal crisis rising along the way, or do you bail him out too soon for the tension to build?

As you review your cards, feel free to shuffle them, insert new ones, or remove any that no longer seem valid. You can further test your writer's intuition by asking a fellow writer (or a reader whose opinion you value) to critique your notecard outline. Challenge him or her to find the holes in your story. You'll find it is far less painful to shred a silly index card than to delete whole, completed chapters that simply don't work.

Having finished crafting your story, you may find your outline easier to work from by transferring it from the cards to a more standard outline form. Either way, as you begin writing, you no longer need to fear facing a blank screen every morning. With your plan in hand and "The End" burned into your brain, you'll be free to let your characters romp, your imagination soar and your prose test new heights of creativity because you've put all the hard stuff behind you.

*So, what is a poor first-time
novelist to do?
Plan.
That's all.*

One Writer's Outline:
Mapping a Mystery

by Marcia Kiser

Have you ever gone on a road trip without a map? Or at least some thing that shows you the best way to get from point A to point B?

Superhighways and interstates are well marked on a good map which draws your eye to them as you calculate the hours and miles to your destination. But look at that map a little more closely. See all those red, green, and brown lines, and all those dotted or hashed lines? Those are secondary and tertiary roads, gravel roads, dirt roads, and county roads—roads that may take a little longer but make interesting side journeys. Yes, you do have to slow down to travel on these smaller roads, but you get to see the scenery—up close and personal and in greater detail than you could ever see them from the interstate.

Writing a novel, whether it's romance, mystery, science fiction or mainstream, is a little like a journey—starting at point A and continuing to point B. Why start writing without a map of some kind—commonly known as the dreaded "outline?"

Editors, agents, and publishers often ask to see chapter outlines, to determine if the story proceeds in an orderly fashion from beginning to end—without getting lost on any side trips. You know you have to do one, so why not start it from the outset?

Outlining, in its simplest form, consists of the standard format you probably used in grammar school—using roman numerals to denote major ideas and listing secondary ideas with A, B, C, etc. Just remembering how it felt to create an outline for a grade is enough to make me break into a sweat. And that may very well be why I have so much trouble outlining myself, even though I see the need for it.

I once heard author Robin Cook on one of the early morning news programs say he uses a large piece of butcher paper tacked to his wall. As scenes occur to him, he jots them on the paper and uses arrows to show the flow, almost like a computer flow chart. Tony Hillerman, author of the Joe Leaphorn/Jim Chee mysteries, says: "I can get a novel written to my satisfaction only by using a much freer form and having faith that—given a few simple ingredients—my imagination will come up with the necessary answers." William Faulkner, literary great, once commented, "I set my characters on the road and walk beside them, listening to what they have to say." Lawrence Block, author of more than thirty mystery and suspense novels, says "It's unarguably true that a writer working from an outline always knows what he originally intended to have happen next. But there's no guarantee it'll work."

Conflicting opinions from some mystery greats. So, what is a poor first-time novelist to do? Plan. That's all. Have a plan in mind of how to get from point A to point B. The simplest, most basic outline is just a map of where you are going.

An outline can be as simple as one line describing a scene, an action, or an event. Or it can be a complex, fifty-page document that covers every event to occur. One method of outlining, used by Kinsey Millhone (Sue Grafton's P. I.), involves 3" x 5" index cards. She notes each fact or scene or bit of information on a card. Should you adopt her method, you can use different colored cards for the crime, the characters, the clues, etc.—however you choose to break things down. You can shuffle the cards into any order you like. A similar strategy is to use sticky notes. Find a large blank surface, and stick your notes on it. You can rearrange them as you see patterns begin to evolve. If you get stuck, move the notes around to see whether you get an inspiration. In addition, many word-processing packages offer outlining capabilities that can make your life easier, if you are a true technocrat.

I have developed my own style of outlining based on what I've learned by writing cozy murder mysteries with continuing characters. For example, I have biography sheets for all of my characters and add to them as the story develops (see "Characters" below). I keep a list of names that occur to me during drives, while buying groceries, or at work, so that there's a place to start when developing new characters. Sometimes, when I'm lucky, a name and a character's description appear in my head and I write them down so as not to lose them. Also, I keep a list of interesting phrases or words that I've heard. All miscellaneous notes go into a loose-leaf notebook that I refer to as "my brain." I'll even jot down potential plot ideas or story lines as they occur to me from reading, dreams, newspapers, or articles.

When I begin a new book, I use a spiral notebook, which is easy to carry everywhere in my purse (and yes, my purse is that big!) I divide the notebook into sections representing elements of the story. Below, I'll describe each section of the outline I make and explain what I do and why.

Chapter and Scene

I tend to think in scenes and chapters, so on a fresh page, I list the name of the scene as the chapter title. On the same page, I list the general time of day, not the exact time. Time of day is often overlooked, but it is important to keep it straight. (You don't want a character going to lunch after another character has eaten dinner—unless, of course, you're writing a flashback.) '

I then describe the scene or where the action is taking place. If this is a new spot, I describe it fully—right down to the spiderwebs in the corners. (You do not have to include everything in your story, but you do want to know the place inside and out so that you can "show" it to your readers.)

I also include weather. For example, if my protagonist is looking for footprints in sandy soil and a thunderstorm is brewing, time becomes pressing, and a sense of urgency is created. Will the footprints be found before the storm hits? Can I feel the blowing dust that comes before the rain hits my protagonist in the face? Can I feel the drop in temperature that normally precedes a storm? Is the murderer going to be inside his living room, watching rain slash at the windows? All these things can enhance a scene, and help build characters.

Anything else that will help develop the scene can and should be noted here. Is there a fire in the fireplace? Is the cat running through the house? Is dinner cooking? Have the weeds in the garden been pulled? In describing my scenes, I try to include each of the five senses, to make it easier to engage the reader.

Characters

Next in my outline, I list the characters I envision. If a new character evolves, I begin a bio sheet right then so that I can update the character as the story develops. My bio sheet includes all the basic information: hair color, eye color, age, height, weight, marital status, and children (if there are a spouse and children, each gets a page). I also include birth date, favorite color, likes, dislikes, and any other pieces of information that will help me flesh out the character. I often include the character's favorite saying, if one occurs to me, to help develop the character's voice.

This sounds like a lot of work, but by writing so many things down, I make characters become real for me. I can hear them in my head and know what clothes they might buy, their favorite kinds of soda, their favorite times of year, their ticks and quirks. They become my friends. Knowing my characters this well helps me "show" them more easily to my future readers.

Each bio sheet is easily updated as the character develops or as I change my mind about particular characteristics. The bio sheet saves time when I need to recall whether a character has a crooked smile over a chipped tooth (and which tooth is chipped).

Action

The next thing I describe is the action that I "expect" to happen. Please note that I said "expect." Nothing in my outline is written in stone. And the "action" section is probably the most nebulous of all the parts of my outline. As the story and characters develop and take on a life of their own, those interesting side trips begin to occur, and I have to follow them. I may wind up lost, with not a clue as to how to get back, or at a dead-end, but, more often than not, I arrive at a valuable scene that adds insight or tension to the plot. If I do lose my way, my trusty outline will help get me back on track.

In the outline for chapter 6 of the book I am currently working on, the action portion looks like this:

1. Raymond tells his story.
2. Clara urges Raymond to go to the police.

3. Raymond runs away after the evening news comes on.
4. Juan and Rachel beg Clara for help.

At this stage in the outlining process, I paint in broad, sweeping strokes, but I have a sense of what might happen in this chapter. I have not decided exactly how I want these things to take place or how they will evolve, but I am envisioning at least these four things in chapter 6.

Purpose

Purpose is the reason for the scene, the reason the actions I've outlined occur. In chapter 6, for example, my purpose is to introduce Raymond. At this point in the story, I go to my bio sheet and sketch in his background, description, etc.—whatever I want the reader to know about him. The second purpose of chapter 6 is to get Clara personally involved in the murder. Since I write cozies with an amateur protagonist, this point is extremely important. The reader has to understand why Clara is going to snoop, and nothing works better than a personal reason. Juan is Clara's friend, a ranch foreman who has worked for her for many, many years. Raymond is Juan's cousin. Juan asks Clara to help Raymond. Clara thus becomes involved—with a valid reason to snoop.

Foreshadowing

In select chapters, I include a category for foreshadowing. If I want to drop a clue that will have later impact, I mention it in this section of my outline, so that I can remember it easily. It might be a piece of gossip overheard that is later recalled. It might be a car that your character later remembers. It might be a jacket that disappeared but is discovered later on. Necessarily, "foreshadowing" is a vague category. Until I get into the story, I may not know exactly what I want to foreshadow. But I try to remember one of the primary rules of mystery writing: "If a gun is shown in the first of the story, it must be fired or explained by the end." A writer can't leave any loose threads. By using a "foreshadowing" category in my outline, I can keep track of those threads and make sure they are finally tied up.

General

Here is where I add anything that I think might add to a chapter. For example, in one of my chapter outlines, I have Clara watching an old movie in the "Action" section. In "General," I list possible movies that she could watch. Elsewhere, if a character is eating, I might want to make a note of the food or the restaurant. If a character is reading, I might make a note of the book. If a character is driving, I might make a note about highway signs. Or I might include what flowers would be in bloom during a particular time of year, or if there is a chance of forest fire. These things can be used to add a special touch to a scene.

As the story progresses, I make notes on my outline of anything that occurs to me while writing: new clues that come to mind, devilish red herrings, or new motivations for characters that can add a twist. This is why I use a spiral notebook: I can carry it with me everywhere and add things to the outline at any time. Subconsciously, writers are always thinking about their stories. Events, ideas, suggestions, characters, scenes, settings, anything can pop into consciousness at any time. I'm prepared; I carry my outline with me.

Sequence and Sticky Notes

The best part is plotting the actual crime and the solution. For that, since it takes considerable work, I abandon my outline, temporarily, and use sticky notes, which I can arrange and re-arrange to my heart's content. Also, I can add or delete things until I have the actual sequence just right, then go back to the outline to record the sequence. This method can be very rewarding, especially if time is a major factor.

I start by listing a sequence of events. Each event gets a different sticky note. I then list the suspects. Each suspect and each action by that suspect gets a note. Then, I start adding times. The sequence of events and the suspect's actions will overlap because, after all, actions occur at specific times. If you have the murder occurring at 8:05, then each one of your suspects should be doing something at 8:05, to help develop an alibi.

In my first novel, a broken watch at the scene of the crime established the time of the murder (later, the readers discover the watch had been deliberately set forward). My cast of characters had to have alibis for this time, and it came down to tracking them almost minute-by-minute. Keeping track of four or five (or more) people, each going different directions, doing their assigned tasks, can be a huge undertaking. But using sticky notes made the job much easier for me.

Again, I update my outline with specific times when they have been determined. When I complete my draft of the book, I update the outline, and I continue to update during the rewriting process. Making notes of everything I change makes the outline a handy reference.

My approach takes a lot of work, but by the time I have finished a story, I have my outline—chapter by chapter. I also have an easy way to write a synopsis by using the action portion of the outline, which can be summarized in two to three sentences. Sometimes I add details to the synopsis, but I already have the basic document.

By using my outline, I have developed my story line, planted my clues, played fair with my future readers, and stayed on track from point A to point B.

Most important, I still have the flexibility, once I've started writing the book, to explore those interesting side roads that all characters love to travel.

How to Write a Seamless Transition

By Eileen Alcorn Workman

In good novel writing, transitions between scenes occur so seamlessly that the reader's enjoyment isn't undermined by a sudden shift in the story. But many aspiring authors, while they study other elements of craft, tend to overlook these subtle connectors. It is perhaps their very "hiddenness" that makes transitions so difficult for most new authors to master.

A transition occurs whenever one self-contained, real-time scene ends and a new scene begins. Most transitions fall into one (but sometimes two or more) of the following categories:

— A time shift, which propels the reader chronologically forward through the story.

— A location shift, which moves the action to a new venue.

— A character shift, which changes who is presently "up on stage."

— A flashback, which reveals important information about a character's history.

Of these four transition types, the most potentially jarring are flashbacks and time shifts, because these force the reader to "lift" himself out of the present scene and to "drop down" in a new time (and often place, as well). Since most readers mentally plant themselves in the shoes of the protagonist and "walk" with him through the story scene by scene, a good writer should strive to preserve that connection through every scene change. Although many books for novice writers discourage the use of flashbacks, a well-placed and well structured flashback need not disrupt your story or disturb your reader. A good rule of thumb when dealing with flashbacks is "had in, had out." Simply put, use the word "had" or "hadn't" in the first sentence of the flashback, then omit the past participle for the balance of the flashback. When the time comes to return to the current action, a final use of the word "had" will cue the reader that the flashback is nearing its end. An example:

> She'd had the very same dream once before, when she was a child. A blue unicorn drinking peacefully from a stream, unaware of any danger until it was accosted by a masked, berobed stranger with empty eye sockets and a bloody butcher knife. The screams of the unicorn awakened her, the same as before. What did it mean, that she'd had the dream again after all these years? She didn't know.

More common than flashbacks are time "warps." The passage of a few hours can sometimes be noted by a simple paragraph change, but suppose that many weeks, months, or even years have passed since the end of your last scene. You as writer are obliged to make your reader aware of any lengthy passage of time if you expect him to make a leap forward with your characters. The simplest way to move past a large block of time is to begin with a fresh chapter. Upon seeing a chapter change, the reader will quickly adjust after a mention of time having passed. If a chapter change isn't possible or practical, another option is to use an extra white space to denote a major shift in the story. A common technique in nonfiction, the white space also has a place in novel writing, although it should be used as sparingly as possible. Hint: the faster the story resumes, the more comfortable a time shift will feel to the reader. Some examples of swift time transitions:

—Three years had passed since Laura last saw Paul....

—Jacob's shoulders had grown hunched, and his hair had thinned....

—Summer faded into fall, which greyed to winter....

How can we shift smoothly from one setting to another and also change the characters currently appearing onstage? The key to a smooth setting and character shift is to avoid telling the reader the mundane details of how a particular character arrived, left, or travelled from point A to point B. By ending one paragraph with the indication of future travel and beginning the next with the destination having already been reached, the writer can swiftly propel the reader from one setting to another. With a few quick brush stroke descriptions of the new scene, the magic is complete—our character and our action take off in a brand-new place. An example:

> ...Michael detested flying. So much did takeoffs and landings terrify him that he was, as always, the last to board when they announced the final call for his flight.
>
> Three Bloody Marys later he was also the first to exit. Feeling too unsteady to rent a car, Michael hailed a cab— he loved that about San Francisco, that cabs were actually available—and struggled to recall the directions to Angela's office.
>
> The woman he adored worked in a big building, one with twenty-four floors that made him dizzy when he looked up. Her bosses kept her locked away in a cubicle on nineteen. She didn't seem pleased when he announced he'd come to rescue her....

Note that both time and location have shifted in the first part of this transition, and that the characters on stage have shifted in the second. For beginning writers, such a major transition might be easier to accomplish with a chapter change or a white space, but you can see how the mention of Michael's trip alerts the reader to his journey and allows the entire shift to be completed in a few quick sentences and with two simple paragraph changes. The more skilled a writer becomes at accomplishing this kind of "invisible" transition, the less jarred the reader is likely to feel when such major shifts occur.

A novel must have conflict, not just in its over-arching idea, but in every single scene.

Pacing Anxiety
Or How To Stop Padding And Plot!

by Caro Clarke

O ne of the great fears of novice writers is that they don't have enough to say. They worry that their chapters are too short and need padding and that their whole novel is going to end up a measly forty-seven pages.

This is pacing anxiety. You are afraid that you don't have enough to write about, and you are almost certainly right. Most novice writers don't have enough plot because they confuse their premise with plot.

For instance, you have an idea for a story: a timid woman called Jenny, feeling that her life is smothered by commitments and duties, decides on a whim to go into the bed-and-breakfast business in Alaska. A good premise. But it's not a plot. So you think of several scenes: Jenny encounters a bear, learns to cook a moose, faces her first Alaskan winter, meets the local Indian guide and his family, encounters a hunky biologist (cue romance!), has hard times, gets a lucky booking, and ends up with a successful business, a new lover, and a sense of achievement. Great material! So you start to write.

No, no, no! You *still* don't have a plot! That's why you have pacing anxiety! You don't know how you're going to turn these scenes into a novel, so you start writing, hoping that somehow the story will grow like Jack's bean stalk. Do you really expect to produce cohesion and structure and density by simply writing what pops into your head every day? A good novel is planned. That means having a structure where things happen for a reason. Your premise implies that Jenny, feeling stifled, heads to Alaska to improve her life. Your plot, therefore, is about a woman who creates a better life for herself by accepting challenge, and everything you write has to develop to this resolution.

Challenge implies battling something, overcoming opposition, and this is the heart of novel writing. Fiction is about challenges that the protagonist either triumphs over or is defeated by (see *Emma* or *Madam Bovary*, for example). A novel must have conflict, not just in its over-arching idea, but in every single scene.

Your premise is merely the novel's opening action. In the example used here, Jenny's first challenge is what to do about a life she has recognized as unfulfilling. You have to show your readers just enough about her life (overbearing father, boring boyfriend, emotionally dependent mother, selfish friends) to make them as thrilled as Jenny is to see the "For sale: large house, Grizzly Bay, Alaska" advertisement, and to approve when she faces the storm of protest and spends her life savings on it. Since a chapter should not have more than three separate pieces of action, getting all this into Chapter One means that there's no need—in fact, no room—for padding. See how easy it is to remove anxiety?

Now you have the rest of the novel to write. You already have those few scenes in mind, but have you put them to the *conflict* test? Where in them will Jenny be in conflict?

First, of course, it will be within herself. She arrives in Grizzly Bay with prejudices, fears, and ignorance. If she is a good person (and she is), she will fight to remove her prejudices. If she is brave, she will face her fears. If she opens herself to change, her ignorance will be dispelled. Fine! Now let's make all that concrete.

Plot an arc of encounters. That face-to-face moment with the bear, for instance, can be when she learns that she is tougher than she thought. During a cold winter night, she could realize that the song of the wolves and the vastness of the starry sky are not terrifying, but beautiful. As you consider Jenny as a person, you will think of more challenges for her. Learning to butcher a moose? Fixing the snowmobile herself? Your novel's premise has assumed a resolution, so you know Jenny will have to have a revelatory moment when she realizes that, because of her initial action (moving to

Alaska), she is a better, happier person. All those scenes of internal conflict will lead inexorably to that revelation. And that provides your structure.

But this novel, because of its premise (Jenny is running a bed-and-breakfast inn, after all, not becoming a hermit), will involve Jenny's meeting new people. You've already thought of a few. Now introduce conflict. Jenny will be having paying guests, a positive wellspring of conflict. She's learning the business while doing it, and some of her guests won't like that. She might make mistakes that give her business a bad reputation, and she'll have to fight it by a publicity drive, sweet-talking travel agents in Anchorage, and so on. All of this is conflict, and it's all action.

She'll be meeting more people than simply her guests. Think about those other characters. The local guide might resent yet another white person moving in, and the hunky biologist will naturally fear the impact of tourism on the fragile ecosystem. Give Jenny an unwelcome neighbor— say, an unmarried teenage mother who's been living in the shack on the property—and you have more than enough opportunities for conflict.

Draw out a sequence of conflicts for each of these characters. Tanu, the local guide, can meet Jenny and warn her that she isn't tough enough to live in his world. Later she helps his wife skin a moose. Tanu's son gets lost and she helps in the search. Now place these "Tanu events" alongside your sequence of Jenny's inner struggles. Start weaving them together. Right after Tanu's warning, Jenny can have her encounter with the bear and realize that she is tougher than she thought. Helping Tanu's wife butcher the moose teaches her the need for cooperation, reveals the wisdom of Native American ways, and banishes her squeamishness forever. It will be while searching for Tanu's lost child that Jenny has to fix her snowmobile herself, and does. All these incidents mean that her final revelation can be, in part, because Tanu and his family have accepted her.

In the same way, the teenage mother, Karyn, who at first tries to drive Jenny away because she fears that Jenny plans to make her homeless, is initially a source of conflict for Jenny. This is resolved when Jenny hires her to work at the bed-and-breakfast. Perhaps it is Karyn, also watching the Northern Lights on that cold winter's night, who opens Jenny's eyes to the haunting beauty of Alaska, weaving two lines of conflict together in one. Jenny's kindness to Karyn impresses Tanu, Mike, and the other townspeople, and shows that accepting the challenge of a new life has made her a better person.

Mike, the biologist, will at first be coldly hostile, but as Jenny listens to him and begins to promote eco-friendly trips to her guests, he thaws. Having learned much about Native needs and attitudes from Tanu's family, Jenny defends Tanu's hunting in the face of Mike's opposition, earning his and the community's respect. During the search for Tanu's son, Mike and Jenny could meet and join forces, and he could see in action the courage she has learned over the past months. The climax could come when Jenny, just ahead of Mike, finds Tanu's son and brings him back to the town, enduring frostbite because she has wrapped the boy in her own parka. It is then, having made a real difference to other people's lives and having lived up to her highest ideals, that Jenny has her revelation.

As you lay each conflict sequence down beside the others, you will see what to blend where, what to reposition, and what can be combined—and combine them you must because you'll have so much story to tell that every scene will have to do double the work! You will find the action easily divisible into fairly equal chunks, and these will be your chapters. (Notice that chapters come at the end, not at the beginning, of the process). You will have lost your anxiety and replaced it with the solid plot of a completed novel.

Write What You Know?

by Eileen Alcorn Workman

*I*n the past few years, I've witnessed a disturbing trend among New York Publishing houses. In order to make books stand out on their lists, many are publicizing the fact that their current legal thrillers are written by ex-lawyers; their police procedurals, by ex-cops; their spy thrillers, by ex-CIA agents. Which is all well and good if your genre happens to match your background, but where does that leave the beginning novelist who doesn't have the proper "qualifications" to make such claims? After all, we're not talking about sex-therapy manuals, diet books, or twelve-step self-help programs here—we're talking fiction. And, by definition, fiction is a product of the author's imagination. It's doubtful that Melville ever tackled a white whale or that Dostoyevsky ever committed a heinous murder; nor was Poe ever buried alive. Yet all these writers produced classic tales that rang of authenticity.

So then, how does a writer combat this new trend if, say, he works as an accountant from nine-to-five? "A day in the life of a CPA" isn't likely to sell many copies, which means most of us must turn our imaginations farther afield than our current mundane careers. It's not easy, especially since we're constantly bombarded with that terribly stifling edict to "write what you know." These words, I believe, are the worst advice a beginning writer can hear.

My response? Whenever I hear some well-meaning but foolish person utter that phrase, I simply smile, nod, then silently add three small words to the statement: "to be true." That's it—the secret to writing authentic works of fiction. Write what you know to be true. So what if you're working on a historic romance and can't time-travel back to visit merry old England in the fourteenth century? You can do in-depth research into the lifestyles, food, and clothing of the period. Police procedurals? It doesn't take a cop to study the hierarchy and standard procedures of the department you're basing your book on. Better yet, go out and spend time with an officer in the field.

I recently completed a novel set in the Florida Everglades, a place I'd visited only briefly, as a child. As part of my writing process, I rented *National Geographic* videos, contacted the National Park Service for maps and information, and purchased coffee-table picture books to help me better envision the setting I was creating. Before completing the novel, I actually traveled to Florida and spent a week hiking and canoeing in the very swamps I was writing about, an experience which gave me the smells and feels and even the authentic mosquito bites to add color and texture to my story.

One important thing I've learned is that most professionals love sharing their knowledge. People like to feel important. It's human nature. So don't be afraid to pick up the phone and identify yourself as a writer in search of information. I've done it a dozen times, and, as scary as it feels sometimes, I have yet to be challenged to "prove" I'm the genuine thing. The fact is, most of the professionals I've turned to for help have bent over backwards to offer me assistance. (It also helps to tell them you'll mention them in your acknowledgments!)

Work at applying your own knowledge and personal insight regarding human behavior to your characters. Make their actions and thoughts ring true, and the rest of the story will follow. Behaviors and emotions are universal; the human condition is an area in which every one of us is an expert.

So, by all means, feel free to plunk your characters down in a fantasy or sci/fi world, or even smack in the middle of a serial killer's universe. Later, if any naysayers challenge your credentials, just smile and tell them you're a card-carrying member of the human race. That ought to shut them right up—particularly if you've written a darn good novel.

Plot Technique:
The Rule Of Three

by t. a. carr

I t may be simplistic to say, "The character's concerns become the story's concerns," but these are what the plot is built upon. As you write your story, the plot will develop patterns. Your job, as the writer, is to recognize and guide them, to strengthen them and make them more coherent. If you build patterns intentionally in your plot, the structure of the story is brought into focus as there is a subtle power in recurrence. One particularly effective method of placing an intentional pattern in the plot is The Rule of Three.

Many children's stories have the Rule of Three as the plot premise. The three little pigs building their houses, Cinderella and the two stepsisters trying on the glass slipper, the three bears discovering their possessions familiar to most of us; each has a situation that occurs three times.

The first time the situation occurs, it is an isolated incident, perhaps providing a risk factor and some conflict. The pig with the straw house doesn't last long against the wolf. Then the second occurrence sets the pattern. The wolf gets the pig with the house made of sticks, as well. Now the reader will feel tension and suspense, and will worry about the pig in the house made of brick. But the third occurrence changes the pattern by going against the outcome of the previous two situations. The third situation breaks the pattern, and we have a winner. The big, bad wolf huffs, and he puffs, but he can't blow down the brick house.

The Rule of Three can provide drama because the reader can experience a character's failure. Let's suppose Charlie Brown is ready to kick the football out of Lucy's hands. He runs and kicks. She moves the ball away. Charlie falls. (I think his shoes and socks come off as well). The second time he tries, he falls again. Then Charlie prepares to kick the ball the third time. If we are following the Rule of Three, something must change on the third attempt. Charlie runs to kick the ball, and Lucy moves it. Charlie moves also and kicks it out of her hands. (She ends up on her back with her shoes and socks off). Had we put Charlie on his back again, the reader would find the situation monotonous and become bored with the story. But by providing three similar situations, the last with significant change, we have suspense, pattern and contrast all in one.

The Rule of Three's uses are obvious. For example, it can be used to direct the reader's attention. Suppose the story of the three pigs is part of a larger work, and suppose it's important to the story to establish that the brick house can withstand the wolf. By using the huff-and-puff scene in the beginning, you can set up the reader to remember later that the wolf can't get in the brick house. The pattern can also be used to prepare for a "big scene." Let's say Charlie Brown is supposed to kick the ball at a school-yard competition. He and Lucy practice twice before the event, with the results mentioned. The first two situations are private, but the competition will be in front of the whole school, including the little "red haired girl" Charlie likes. We lead Charlie, by the pattern, to a big scene, and the stakes and the tension are high. The Rule of Three can make a scene's meaning more clear to the reader. The reader knows what a character has gone through to get where they are in the story.

The Rule of Three is relatively easy to drop into your story and makes for an interesting plot. Keep the situations highly visible so the reader discovers the pattern without being told. Don't have a character state, "I do believe I've experienced this before." Incident number one shows the situation, two sets the pattern, and three breaks the pattern.

Recommended Reading on the Rule of Three:
Dibell, Ansen, *Plot*, Writer's Digest Books. 1988, ISBN 0-89879-303-3

Point Of View

Point of View
Or Choosing A Storyteller

by P. J. Woodside

*P*oint of view is one element of a story that must be selected by the writer. It cannot be allowed to happen spontaneously or haphazardly, and it must be chosen before the writing of a story can begin. Each possible point of view must be examined for its advantages and disadvantages for a particular story. Only then can the writer make the best choice.

It's helpful to think of the different points of view as in a circle, each connected to the others, rather than as separate entities. At the top of the circle would be the omniscient point of view (all-knowing or God-like). One-third around the circle, to the right, would be third person. Two-thirds around, moving back toward the omniscient, is first person.

From the omniscient point of view, any detail or thought about any character, place, or event can be told—the voice is often that of the author, who knows all. This voice can either tell the story without calling attention to itself (no authorial intrusion) or reflect the story-telling roots of the novel by speaking directly to readers from time to time (you get my drift, dear reader?). This authorial voice has fallen from favor with the rise of movies and television, where the storyteller's identity is no longer a necessary element of relating a story.

From the omniscient point of view, the author has the advantage of being able to move freely from one character to another, telling any part of the story she wishes to share with the reader. What may be lost are immediacy and focus. It may be difficult for a reader to sympathize with any particular character if there are too many with well-rounded features and complicated lives to choose from (or maybe they all lack such fullness—another pitfall). The charm of omniscience for the reader is being able to watch the characters play out their faults and foibles as an observer looking on. The danger for the writer is in not being able to create a focus to keep the reader's attention.

The third-person point of view is often called limited omniscient or third-person limited. It's clearly related to omniscient in pronoun use (the use of "he" or "she" in reference to all characters). From third person, the telling of the story is limited to the experiences of one main character rather than those of a whole world of characters. An authorial voice is still present, in a narrowed and focused form. Usually, only the thoughts of the main character may be told, and time and place are limited by that character's presence.

Third-person limited gives a sense of focus often missing from omniscient stories; it solves the problem of too much "I-ness" that is sometimes found in first-person stories. But it sacrifices a sense of intimacy. We never truly know who is speaking to us in a third-person limited story—a storyteller? An author? Certainly not a character. This point of view is often a good choice for beginning writers, however, because it has a nice balance of limits and freedoms without spiraling into confession.

From the first-person point of view, only one character's perceptions of the story-world may be related, and then only in the limited capacity of that character. A demented character may be untrustworthy; an unintelligent character may be ignorant of necessary bits of information. Unlike third-person limited, however, first person requires that the main character tell the story directly; the reader need not wonder who is speaking. First person has risen in popularity with the modern shift of emphasis toward the individual. It makes possible a personal kind of style.

The limitations of first person—nothing beyond that character's consciousness may be related—are made up by immediacy and focus. A reader cannot help putting herself in the character's shoes, perhaps even beginning to understand a character who is demented or stupid or monstrous. The danger of first person is self-indulgence on the part of the main character— too many "I" sentences, too much self-pity. The best first-person stories focus outward rather than inward, giving signs of inner conflict through actions, rather than explanations.

Both first and third person are related to omniscient; in a sense. they are extensions of it. In third person the authorial voice is gone, but the storyteller is retained (in the "he" and "she"), allowing distance. In first person, the authorial voice remains but is limited to one person's consciousness—that of the character relating the story. What's lost is the sense of a story being woven for the reader. Instead, the reader becomes a voyeur, watching the life of the "I."

A couple of unusual points of view fall between these three main ones. Between first and third is second. Second-person point of view is seldom used by writers, with good reason: It rarely works. Second person replaces what would be the "he" or the "I" of a story with "you." Consequently, the reader may feel dragged into the story as a participant. Though "you" implies the reader's presence and participation in the story, what's happening is being dictated by someone else.

Second-person point of view is more an experiment than a useful tool. It usually involves pronoun repetition and negates the storytelling voice to the extent that it ruins the experience for the reader. Still, it's a less-explored option that may prove useful in some important way in the future.

Between omniscient and first person falls plural first person, or the group "we." Faulkner uses this point of view in his story "A Rose for Emily," in which the teller is not an "I" and not an all-knowing author, but a collective "I"—the "we" who know this story and all about the town but not beyond it. This point of view can be used for good effect in certain circumstances.

Ultimately, each point of view is an extension of the storyteller sitting by the fire, suspending disbelief through images created by words, lighting eyes and lifting hearts with nothing more than her voice and brain. Whatever point of view a writer chooses, she must remember this: The story cannot be told without the voice, but the job of the storyteller is to make people remember the story, not the voice.

To write in first person successfully, you must become your main character for the duration of the story.

"I" Is Not Me

by Tricia Bush

First Person Is Natural

First-person point of view is the most natural way to write. First person is the way we talk to others about our day; it is the way we speak. We write our diaries and journals in first person. We gossip in first person. We conduct business in first person. We brag about the fish we caught in first person. We probably wrote our first school paper in first person, as in "What I Did on My Summer Vacation." When we tell someone about our day or our summer vacation, we are ourselves. First person (the "I") in fiction is entirely different.

So why are there so many writing teachers who advise against writing in the first person? Why do they say it is very difficult, when it is something we do naturally?

The Plot Is Your Stage

Think of yourself as an actor in a play. If you are playing Romeo, you won't slouch onto the stage in baggy jeans and yell to Juliet, "Hey, Babe, let's get it on." That might be the way a real contemporary boy would do it. An actor, on the other hand, shows up in those silly tights, speaks the lines that were written for Romeo, and becomes Romeo for the time that he is on the stage, spouting poetry as if all people expressed themselves poetically.

Getting Into Character And Staying There

To write in first person successfully, you must become your main character for the duration of the story. You must get into that character's head and stay there. In *Moby Dick,* the first line says, "Call me Ishmael." It does *not* say, "Call me Herman Melville." The author is saying that we are going to see the story through the eyes of this character. All of the events that follow will be filtered through this character's eyes, and mind, and heart. We trust the author to keep the fictional dream intact by staying within this character throughout the entire journey.

Character consistency is harder than it may look because writers are human. We have bad days. We have differing moods. We are sometimes in pain. In order to write in first person, we must set aside all of those everyday experiences. The snow that is piled three feet deep in the driveway, the fact that a family member wrecked the car, or the call from the IRS threatening an audit must be forgotten while the character glories in a gorgeous summer day. And we can't fake it. We must feel it, or our writing won't ring true.

The Pleasures of First Person

There are some wonderful things about writing in first person.

It is the most immediate and intimate of voices. It is instantly convincing. With the first words of a story, the author creates a distinctive voice and personality for a character. We don't have to worry about how much interior monologue we are writing because, in essence, the whole story is told in interior monologue. Flashbacks become natural as part of the plot. We can telescope time in and out, we can tell the story as if it were happening right now, we can tell it as if it happened to a different (younger) "I" person in a different time and place, or we may use any combination of past and present.

The first-person narrator can be one who tells the story about him or herself, or one who tells a story about another person or persons. In Charles Dickens' *David Copperfield,* which begins "I am born," the main character goes on to ruminate about whether or not he will be the hero of the story of his life. There is no question about who the central character is going to be. In *Moby Dick,* Ishmael may be telling the story, but no one would say that he is the main character, although he is (and the first-person narrator must always be) a part of the story. (Otherwise, he is an extra person, hanging around expressly to tell the story, in which case the author could let him go home and simply tell the story in third person.)

Many mysteries are written in first person because wonderful suspense is created when we are forced to uncover the clues and solve the puzzle right along with the detective.

The Pitfalls of First Person

1. The most difficult thing about writing in first person is staying *in voice*—that is, staying within that character's *personality* (no matter how much the author wants to describe something in his own voice) and maintaining the character's energy for the long haul. The story falls apart when the character loses his *voice* and begins to sound like a different person or just anyone on the street.

2. The first-person narrator cannot know what other people are thinking. All of the other characters must reveal themselves to the reader through dialogue and through actions heard and seen by the first-person character. This is much as it is in real life. We never really know what others are thinking; we know only what they tell us or how they act. But an author does know what the other characters are thinking—the trick is to make it seem as if he doesn't.

3. All information must come through the first-person character before it gets to the reader. How the character gathers that information is sometimes difficult to make clear. First-person narrators have been known to eavesdrop, read other people's letters and diaries, and do other sneaky things in their efforts to get what is needed. This is a problem particularly when the first person is in the present, as in a mystery story. It is not so much of a problem when the first-person narrator is speaking of the past.

4. The first-person narrator must live to tell the story. The loss of suspense is one of the pitfalls of first person, especially in a thriller. The question "Will he survive?" has already been answered. For that reason, most thrillers and horror stories are written in third person, as the

author doesn't want the reader to know whether or not the character survives.

5. Finally there is the difficulty of describing the "I" character. Looking in a mirror and thinking about how she or he looks is out unless the author is extremely clever. The reader must come to *see* the first-person narrator through dialogue and/or interior monologue. And the information must seem to come naturally. The author cannot describe the first person as if she or he was out-of-body: i.e., "I flipped my greasy black hair out of my eyes, which shone like emeralds in the dark." Rather, a writer must approach description obliquely and with subtlety. For instance, the dialogue might include "Your hair sure could stand a good wash," from another character. The color of the hair and the color of the eyes aren't mentioned, but they can be inserted elsewhere in similar fashion.

And So

If you write in first person with skill and passion and if you keep in mind its limitations while exploring the range of your voice, your character will live and breathe for the reader as she or he does for you. And if you have done your job well, the reader will make friends with your character and remain a friend throughout the story.

Melville, Herman. *Moby Dick,* Bantam Classics, 1981 (reissue), ISBN: 0553213113

Dickens, Charles. *David Copperfield,* Penguin USA, 1997 (Paper Reprint), ISBN: 0140434941

Choosing Your Storyteller: The Point-of-View Character

by Elizabeth Delisi

Point of view, or viewpoint, is the perspective from which your story is told. There are three standard viewpoints you can choose from when planning your book: first-person, third-person limited, and third-person omniscient. In order to choose the best viewpoint character for your story, try asking yourself the following questions: Who has the most to lose, or to gain, in the story? Who is the targeted reader most likely to identify with? Which character's voice would best suit the story? Which character is most likely to be in on all the important events? Which character needs to grow or change most? When you've answered these questions, you've found the viewpoint character for your story. In many cases, the point-of-view style and character are up to the author; however, some genres have a "traditional" viewpoint that it's best to adapt, especially if you're a beginner.

Many mysteries are written from the first-person point of view. The viewpoint character is usually the "detective," whether professional or amateur, who will ultimately solve the crime. This strategy works well for the mystery genre because it allows the reader to discover evidence and clues along with the main character while not having the solution revealed too early.

The tradition of the first-person narrator in a mystery may have begun with Edgar Allen Poe, credited by many with writing the first detective story. In "The Murders In The Rue Morgue," Poe's narrator tells the story of his acquaintance with Monsieur C. Auguste Dupin, and we see Dupin solve a particularly grisly double murder through the narrator's eyes. Dupin and the narrator form a Sherlock Holmes/Dr. Watson duo, with Dupin doing the sleuthing and the narrator always two steps behind.

> At these words a vague and half-formed conception of the meaning of Dupin flitted over my mind. I seemed to be upon the verge of comprehension, without power to comprehend...My friend went on with his discourse.

"The Murders In The Rue Morgue"

Gothic romance novels frequently employ the first-person narrator, and that tradition has carried over into romantic suspense, as well. The viewpoint character is always the heroine. The first- person mode allows the author to "hold back" important pieces of information from the reader while enabling the reader to share the heroine's emotional reactions to the events in the story.

In *Lament For A Lost Lover*, Philippa Carr firmly establishes the heroine's voice and viewpoint in the first sentence: "Although I did not realize it at the time, the day Harriet Main came into our household was one of the most significant of my life." We immediately know that the narrator is intelligent and astute, but that a great deal of information was withheld from her during the events she's about to reveal.

First person has several advantages. It tends to give a sense of reality to the story because the events unfold in front of the reader as the viewpoint character experiences them. The first-person narrator is considered to be an "unreliable narrator"—in other words, you can't necessarily believe everything the narrator says because his or her perspectives are colored by personal views, feelings, emotional problems, and experiences. This bias can be an advantage in a mystery or suspense story, where you want to mislead the reader intentionally. First person can also help the reader identify more strongly with the viewpoint character.

The biggest disadvantage of using first person is that you can tell the story only from the point of view of one character. Anything that narrator doesn't know, hasn't seen, or hasn't been told, cannot appear in the story. Physical and psychological descriptions of the viewpoint character must be handled delicately in order to be believable. You can't get away with "I stared at my reflection in the mirror and noticed my long, wavy auburn hair, my creamy skin, and my pink rosebud lips." But, at the same time, the narrator must be a fully fleshed-out character that the reader can identify with, or you'll lose the reader's interest and credulity.

In today's fiction, third person viewpoint is used most often. Third person can work in two ways: as third person limited, where the story is written from the point of view of one character only, or as third-person omniscient, where the reader sees the story from more than one character's point of view.

Katherine Anne Porter uses third-person limited in her short story, "The Jilting Of Granny Weatherall." Granny's voice comes through clearly in every sentence.

> She flicked her wrist neatly out of Doctor Harry's pudgy careful fingers and pulled the sheet up to her chin. The brat ought to be in knee breeches. Doctoring around the country with spectacles on his nose! "Get along now, take your schoolbooks and go. There's nothing wrong with me."

In "The Short Happy Life Of Francis Macomber," Ernest Hemingway chooses third-person omniscient in order to show the story from the points of view of Francis Macomber, his wife Margaret, and his safari guide, Wilson. Here's an example from each:

> ① [Wilson] had decided now that to break would be much easier. He would eat, then, by himself and could read a book with his meals. They would eat by themselves. He would see them through the safari on a very formal basis—what was it the French called it? Distinguished consideration— and it would be a damn sight easier than having to go through this emotional trash.

> ② But that night after dinner and a whisky and soda by the fire before going to bed, as Francis Macomber lay on his cot with the mosquito bar over him and listened to the night noises, it was not all over. It was neither all over nor was it beginning. It was there exactly as it happened with some

parts of it indelibly emphasized and he was miserably shamed at it. But more than shame he felt cold, hollow fear in him. The fear was still there like a cold slimy hollow in all emptiness where once his confidence had been and it made him feel sick.

③ From the far corner of the seat Margaret Macomber looked at the two of them. There was no change in Wilson. She saw Wilson as she had seen him the day before when she had first realized what his great talent was. But she saw the change in Francis Macomber now.

The advantages of third-person narration are many. In third person, a character can be described as handsome or terrified without being made to sound immodest or overly dramatic. Third person may be preferable to first person for a character who would not be adept with words and thus wouldn't be likely or able to tell his own story. It also works with an initially unsympathetic character, giving the reader a chance to get to know the character before deciding to identify with him.

Third-person omniscient allows the reader to see into the mind of several characters when such is necessary to the forward movement of the story. Thus, in a romance, the reader can view the developing relationship from the points of view of both the heroine and the hero. In a horror novel, the reader can feel the main character's terror while also experiencing the twisted mind of the villain.

With both forms of third person, you are free to move the story around in time and space. You can also allow the reader to see events transpiring that the main character doesn't see. This strategy can heighten suspense and reader involvement; the reader wants to shout, "Don't go down to the basement!" because he knows the killer is lurking there although the hero is unaware.

Third-person omniscient must be handled carefully, or you will lose credibility. If you jump around from one character's point of view to another (often called "head-hopping") too often, you may lose the focus of your story. You risk not having a main character at all, or the reader may not identify with the main character because you jump around so often. Your story may become boring or confusing if you include too much information. If the reader questions, "Who is it who can see into all these minds?"

then you're in trouble: he has stopped "living" the story and realizes he is reading something contrived.

Whether you tell your story from the hero's point of view, the heroine's or the villain's, and whether you choose first person, third-person limited or third-person omniscient, make sure your point-of-view characters consistently engage the reader's interest and sympathy. With compelling characterization, you can't go wrong.

Poe, Edgar Allen. *The Works of Edgar Allan Poe*. Longmeadow Press, 1983, ISBN: 0681270659

Carr, Philippa. *Lament For A Lost Lover*. Fawcett Books, 1985 (reissue), ASIN: 0449207714

Porter, Katherine Anne. "The Jilting Of Granny Weatherall." In *The Heath Introduction to Fiction*. D.C. Heath and Company, 1984, ISBN: 0669064440

Hemingway, Ernest. "The Short Happy Life Of Francis Macomber." In *An Introduction to Literature: Fiction, Poetry, Drama*, edited by Sylvan Barnet, Little, Brown and Company, 1971

Settings

Use Of Setting To Indicate Character

by P. J. Woodside

All good writers know to avoid adjectives whenever possible. That's "telling" and we're supposed to be "showing." Yet, revealing all the subtleties of a character without creating a grocery list for your reader can be a challenge. One good way to indicate a character's mood or state of mind is through setting details. By this I mean not only the surroundings—beach, bedroom, or office—but also the props of setting, the details that fill in a scene for the reader. In this way details do double duty—they set both a physical and emotional scene for the reader.

For example, in a story I wrote of a woman feeling overwhelmed by her circumstances, readers are told of "two garden plots of wilting tomato plants and puny cucumbers where water from the garden hose wouldn't reach." On the surface it is simply a detail, but for the reader it sets the mood and tells something about the character. If my protagonist had been a fighter, I might have made the plants full and healthy despite the lack of rain. If she had been an optimist, I might have described the plants as struggling to hold up their heads and then have her go off and give them water right away. As it is, my character sits and looks at the plants but is too absorbed in her mental anguish to even consider taking care of them.

Later in the same story, when my protagonist feels threatened by a woman named Molly, this description follows: "Molly turned quickly, one glass in each hand like weapons." Though the story is told in third-person, the identification of lemonade glasses as weapons reflects the protagonist's state of mind. She feels attacked. Another image of Molly—clinking the glasses together in one hand, for example, or holding them close to her breast—would have created an entirely different mood.

Setting also indicates the tension in the following passage from another novel in which I wrote about a father who must leave his family to serve in Vietnam. The daughter describes the drive to the airport:

> The whole car was quiet, the whole city seemed quiet. A sort of spell had fallen over everyone, especially my mother, and it seemed too sacred for our voices. When a car next to us sputtered, we all jumped.

Again, setting indicates the mood and state of mind of several of the characters.

In another of my stories, told in first person, setting details indicate a changed relationship between the protagonist and her childhood friend. As the story progresses, the house of her friend grows less and less appealing. In the beginning she notes "the large, clean kitchen, the shining table, the wallpaper with pink teakettles." Later, she watches her friend "probe her toes inside a break in the linoleum." Then, the protagonist "looked at one of the pink kettles in the wallpaper. It was misaligned—its spout projected from the bottom instead of the top." And finally, "the wood around the sink dipped, beginning to sag—it looked as if it would fall through any minute." These details, noticed gradually through the course of the story, reveal more than the protagonist is willing to tell about her feelings for her friend.

Setting can play an even larger role in indicating character when it provides conflict in the story. In another example from my own writing, a woman intent on keeping control of her life is faced with uncontrollable events. A paragraph of a weather change indicates her struggle:

> The rain begins. She runs from room to room pulling down the windows, and when she gets to the study she finds puddles already spreading across the floor. The rain here comes fast, hard, like just-melted hail. Liv works to keep the dry in, but nothing helps. Last week she threw out a box of envelopes glued shut by the humidity. Mildew multiplies

on everything: the food, the walls, the curtains. Even the pillows.

The setting in this story is an integral part of the character's transformation. The reader does not have to be told that Liv finds the chaos of normal life alarming and distressful. The setting tells it. In another short passage from the same story, the setting details and a few actions of the protagonist make clear her state of mind as the tension builds:

> Liv tries to see the swamp between the trees, tries to see Andy. She takes off for the edge of the water. She follows his canoe path, mud sucking at her boots. She reaches the swamp but she can't see very far, and she can't see Andy. The cypress trees stand still against the rain; the water swirls around them.

No mention of anxiety, worry or distress is necessary here. The weather, the swamp, tells it all. Setting, then, is not merely a backdrop. It is integral to a story. The concrete details a writer chooses must do double-duty, they must give something more to the reader than merely a picture. Next time you're stuck as to how to define a character or express a changing mood, look to the scenery. As a picture is worth a thousand words, an image can be worth a thousand adjectives.

Using Setting To Invite Reader Participation

by Amy Kay Watson

When you write, you create worlds. Perhaps the world you create is one that looks and acts so much like our own that you feel as if we already know it. Nonetheless, you are creating a new world. Readers don't know what kind of world it is until they start reading. Maybe they read the title, or the blurb and the quotes on the back cover, or a review in the newspaper. All this may be enough to tip them off. Most of the time, though, readers won't automatically understand the world you have created. You must describe it.

I used to hate reading the descriptive passages in books. When I was in ninth grade, I read *Silas Marner*, and decided that, if I ever wrote a book, I wouldn't use *any* description. Nevertheless, action without description is bland and lifeless, even if it is punctuated with active verbs. Observe the difference in these two passages:

No description:
> Winnie decided to look in the wood for a source of some music she'd heard the night before. She saw a toad and said, "See? I told you I'd be here first thing in the morning!"

Description:

> The wood was full of light, entirely different from the light she was used to. It was green and amber and alive, quivering in splotches on the padded ground, fanning into sturdy stripes between the tree trunks. There were little flowers she did not recognize, white and palest blue; and endless, tangled vines; and here and there a fallen log, half-rotted but soft with patches of sweet green-velvet moss. (Natalie Babbitt, *Tuck Everlasting*)

When I read the second paragraph, I think to myself, "Yes, of course, I've been in woods just like that...all the time when I was a child." Other readers might find it interesting because they have never had the opportunity to walk in a small wood. In contrast, readers won't react much at all to the first paragraph, other than to ask, "Why is she talking to a toad?" Even though I know the wood Babbitt is describing, I have a much clearer (and more pleasant) picture in my mind than I would have had if she'd simply written "an average wooded area."

How can we invite an empathetic response from our readers? Try the following:

1. Do everything you can to get yourself into the setting.

Get there physically if you can. When Alice Walker was getting ready to write *The Color Purple*, she actually moved three or four times until the characters she had conjured up felt comfortable. They did not belong in San Francisco or Atlanta. It was only when she moved into a cabin in some wilderness that Celie started talking to her and telling her the story. The setting was right. Now, if you are writing fantasy or science fiction, and the world you are creating doesn't have any physical counterparts here on our planet, then do everything you can to get yourself there mentally. Make collages, paint pictures, draw diagrams, collect sound effects, and whip up strange concoctions in your kitchen. Add as much detail as you possibly can so you can see, hear, smell, taste, and *feel* your new world.

2. Act.

Or, I should say, interact. Whenever possible, take on the role of your point-of-view character and experience what that character experiences. Does the character have to run through city streets? Try it. Does the character have to take the bus from Baltimore to Altoona? Find out what it is like. See the world through his or her eyes. Be like the stereotypical actor who is researching for an upcoming role. Put your body where the body of the character will be. Do enough research to find out what the character will see and experience so you know what to try to experience yourself. Is your point-of-view that of an astronaut? Go to a theme park and experience G-forces and take simulation rides. You get the idea.

3. Take notes.

Note-taking has to be the most important aspect of writing. Everywhere you go, take copious notes. I have found that a journal just does not work for this sort of thing. Little scraps of paper work best, because I'm pretty sure to have one with me, whether I'm waiting on a customer, going to the bathroom, or riding Skull Caverns at Six Flags. If you choose this method, bring the scraps to your writing desk and organize them there. Work them into your writing. The other day at work, I wrote down, "Low, ominous clouds, dark and moving fast, like billows of black smoke in the sky—" because a storm was moving through. I saw it, I described it, and I wrote it down so I would not lose the image. It was a unique sight. I had never seen clouds like that before. Of course, I will not necessarily use this description as is, but it is enough to remind me of how they looked so I can describe them at the right time.

4. Write the description.

When your character experiences whatever-it-is, you now know enough to be able to tell us all about it: what does the character see? What does the character hear? smell? taste? feel? The more details you give, the more you will help the reader to connect with the scene.

Babbitt, Natalie. *Tuck Everlasting*. Farrar Straus & Giroux, 1986 (reprint), ISBN: 0374480095

Needless Words

Good writers do not hem and
haw, repeat information,
or bore readers.

The Art Of The Unspoken:
Saying More By Describing Less

by Caro Clarke

Kelly, a newscaster, is visiting a small town months after a fire has swept through the local nursery school. She strikes up a conversation with a woman called Pat and discovers that Pat is the town's news reporter. The conversation continues:

> "You must have been the one to cover that big fire a few months back," Kelly said.
>
> Pat's mouth tightened to a thin line. "Yes," she said in a constricted voice.
>
> Poised on the verge of·asking further questions about the tragedy, Kelly hesitated when she saw Pat's reluctance to speak further and, instead of the question she intended to ask, quickly substituted, "So, how long have you been working as a reporter for the *Bugle*?"

In this section, we see two characters interacting and learn something about them. Pat has been traumatized by her experience and is reluctant to talk about it. Kelly is empathetic to other people's moods and does not push in against someone's distress. Two sensitive people, yet the language is not sensitive. It clunks against our heads like a lead pipe. The writer has told us too much.

The purpose of clean, lean, stylish prose is to tell a story in a satisfying way. Good writers do not hem and haw, repeat information, or bore readers. Instead, they draw readers into the story, letting them feel the action viscerally.

Good writing is like Occam's razor, achieving in the fewest possible words the greatest possible meaning. Writing well requires removing everything unnecessary and achieving precision through combining *what* is happening with the *way* it is happening.

If you are a genius, you achieve this sort of graceful prose in your first draft. If you are merely human, you achieve it by rethinking, refining, and rewriting. You work until nothing else can be cut or altered without risking the full meaning of the content or damaging the narrative flow.

Let's look at the dialogue above. How do you turn that mediocre prose into dynamic language? You start by pruning. Here is the same passage with some padding removed:

> "You must have been the one to cover that big fire here."
> Pat's mouth tightened. "Yes."
> About to launch further questions, Kelly hesitated when she saw Pat's reluctance to speak. Instead of the question she intended to ask, she quickly substituted, "So, how long have you been working for the *Bugle*?"

This rewrite tells us what the first version did, but with fewer words. The passage reads more smoothly, yet you see that your work is not yet done. You must cut more and rewrite that clumsy last section.

> "You must have been the one to cover that big fire."
> Pat's mouth tightened. "Yes."
> Kelly saw Pat's reluctance to speak and, instead of the question she had intended to ask, quickly substituted, "So, how long have you been working for the *Bugle*?"

The action is now starting to get close to "real time," the actual pace of a real conversation, but you sense that you can do better still. You have pruned; now you must combine. Pat is laconic. Her "yes" changes the direction of Kelly's questions. Why not let the reader feel the impact of the question? It doesn't need the prop of the preceding words. You cut those words. You also consider Kelly's first question. Is that how she would say it, or did you write it that way because you thought we wouldn't "get it" and so slipped in a little elucidation? Trust us. We get it.

> "You must have covered that fire."
> "Yes."

Now that this first part makes us feel the impact of Pat's monosyllabic response, the last sentence feels sloppy and too long. It takes us longer to read it than it does Kelly to think it. You want to show the quickness of Kelly's response in the quickness of your writing style:

> Kelly sensed Pat's reluctance to speak. Instead of her intended question, Kelly quickly substituted, "So, how long have you been working for the *Bugle*?"

You are still describing too much. We have already seen Pat's obvious reluctance in her terse "yes," so Kelly seems half a pace behind us. Then we have to wait two whole clauses to see Kelly's supposedly quick, sensitive change of direction. Kelly's response has to be as adroit a change of direction for the reader as it is for her. You rewrite, and finally *you* get it:

> "You must have covered that fire."
> "Yes," said Pat, in a way that made Kelly ask instead, "So, how long have you been at the *Bugle*?"

Your reader, like your character, turns on a dime and heads in a different direction.

By thinking about what is happening and mirroring that action in your style, you have stripped out all superfluity and made the passage a better reading experience. You have moved into the action instead of describing it.

You don't have to spell everything out, hit every nail on the head, cross every "t" and dot every "i." We get it.

Walking The Writing Line:
The Difference Between Enough and Too Much

by Eileen Alcorn Workman

What constitutes too much description or information in a piece of work might seem merely a stylistic choice. However, whether one prefers the minimalist style of Hemingway or the lush and layered prose of F. Scott Fitzgerald, some basic rules of writing always apply. Let's examine three common ways that writers impart information: by making a declarative statement, by foreshadowing, and by describing. We'll focus on when "enough" becomes "too much" in each case.

A declarative statement, as in "Andrea hated Friday mornings," reveals specific detail. A good writer can challenge himself and delight his reader by layering into such sentences truths or falsehoods, hidden meanings or red herrings. Examine the work of many beginning writers, however, and you're likely to find subtle declarative statements immediately followed by sentences that overtly restate the message. Writers use this "double dip" approach because they don't fully trust in their ability to communicate, but the result is always "too much."

Here's an example of a double declarative:

> The sun dropped below the distant hills as magenta faded
> to black. Night had fallen.

Note how both sentences say the same thing—one in a lush, descriptive way and the other as a simple statement of fact. To strengthen your work, examine your declarative passages for just such double statements and keep the one that works best with the surrounding sentences.

Foreshadowing, a second way of communicating information, is the subtle placement of "hints" about the outcome of a story. In hindsight, these statements can be remembered and recognized as signs that point to an inevitable conclusion.

Here's an example:

> The decaying manor loomed at the end of an overgrown drive, its windows shuttered and its brick walls snuffing out the hum of the distant highway. Silent and brooding, the manor kept watch over its surrounding peat bogs and bug-laden swamps, as it had for the past two miserable centuries.

Right off the bat, we realize this isn't a happy house, and that bad things are likely to happen here. The sentence doesn't telegraph or announce any certain impending horror, but it certainly sets a bleak mood and tone for the story. However, foreshadowing can become too much (and too obvious) when it shifts from "hinting" to "announcing" what will follow, as in the following:

> Anthony, the manor's new owner, whistled as he opened the door. Had he known he was embarking on the last awful hours of his life, his whistles might well have been screams.

Such heavy-handed tactics occasionally show up in the works of even the best writers. (The author might as well stick his head over the top of the page and give a wink to his startled reader.) To locate any messages you may have telegraphed in your own work, seek out words and phrases that appear to address the reader directly, interrupting the flow of the story. The most flagrant (and horrible) telegraphing phrase is "little did he know," but there are many others—"if only," "unfortunately," and "unbeknownst," to name a few. Delete these phrases whenever you see them, and substitute a more subtle form of foreshadowing.

A third method of imparting information is through description. By placing adjectives and adverbs strategically, the writer paints a colorful image in the reader's mind. But too many adjectives and adverbs will clutter a sentence. To determine whether your descriptions are overdone, ask yourself if you've conveyed a single, solid image in the sentence, or if you've confused things by attempting to create a multiplicity of images.

> Ripples expanded across the lake, scattering glints of sunlight like so many diamonds.

In this example, a single, unifying image—light dancing upon an undulating lake—is painted.

> A thousand tiny, wind-driven ripples skittered merrily across the cool, wide lake, playfully snatching up brilliant glints of light and then scattering them furiously like a fistful of diamonds along the water's mirrored, deep blue, and impenetrable surface.

The images above are so thickly layered that no single image dominates. The resulting chaos of description creates fatigue in the mind of a reader, not unity of feeling. A good rule of thumb is to select a single noun or verb to modify, then stick to a single modifying clause. You'll note in the first example that not a single adjective or adverb is used to convey the image; rather, active verbs and strong nouns have been chosen instead.

If, after editing your work, you still have doubts about whether your description is overdone, follow the rule that "less is more" and you'll likely do just fine.

*Editing during creation often leaves
our writing mechanically disciplined
but artistically lifeless.*

Slack Attack: Put Your Writing On A Word Diet

by Rodney Lewis Merrill

S lack is pandemic in nonfiction writing. Little wonder. Many of us began padding our writing in middle school to meet misguided word-length requirements, and when we got away with it, padding became our standard for future academic papers. An empty phrase here, reiteration there, and voila! The word requirement is met. I was so "good" at it that my college papers averaged ninety pages or longer. And I was rewarded for it.

My first writing assignments for newspapers and magazines paid, you guessed it, by the word, the inch, or the page. Self-editing was unprofitable. But editors weren't as easily fooled as schoolteachers. I couldn't just patter and repeat myself. I learned that, in journalism, you pad with quotes, sidebars, and other tangential material. Judging by the number of puffy books on the market today, an analogous impetus rules the book market, too.

There's another kind of padding, though, that is unrelated to tricking overlords and paymasters. Tired and confused sentences often bespeak a tired and confused mind. We grow gabby when we are addled, writing in excess to convince ourselves we know what we're talking about. We babble.

Streamlining is so important in aerodynamics that the aviation industry pays very nice wages to workers responsible for polishing and buffing the planes to a high gloss. A glossy plane builds less resistance and attracts less hindering debris. In writing, polishing and buffing has a similar role.

Highly polished writing is streamlined; it's compressed, condensed, and concentrated. It's sleek. It builds less resistance and attracts less hindering debris.

Put your writing on a word diet. Aspire to brevity, and clarity will follow. Strive for clarity and words will fall away like autumn leaves browned and shriveled by superfluity. Lust for both brevity and clarity and the stinkiest of first drafts will soar toward pulchritude.

General Strategies

Don't worry about wordiness while writing the rough draft. Adhere to Anne Lamott's admonition: you must be willing to write really stinky first drafts. Human beings capable of rendering first drafts that are the equal of last drafts are wonderful and precious anomalies. For me, and for other less godlike writers, creation and perfection are disparate stages of the writing process. Editing during creation often leaves our writing mechanically disciplined but artistically lifeless. For us, perfection, when it's possible, is achieved through revision.

Revise when you are fresh. Because we tend to babble when we're stumped, assume that the troublesome passages you tried to *fix* during the first writing need the most trimming and tightening. Hack at them as if they were berry brambles overtaking your flower garden. Below are some good places to start.

Specific Tactics

1. Contracting two or more closely related sentences into one. (Of course, you must judge each sentence construction within the context of the larger work. Sometimes structural repetition is used for effect. Generally, though, an essay composed entirely of short sentences, or long ones, is monotonous.)

> ⬤ Slack: The editor was concerned about writing problems. They were pretty typical. Typical problems include spelling and grammar, tone and voice, setting, and sense of place.

> ⬤ Taut: The editor is concerned about the typical writing problems: spelling and grammar, tone and voice, setting, and sense of place.

⟶Slack: Internet power has been aggregating. This has dampened the once widely held hope among "Net heads" for the emergence of an egalitarian utopia.

⟶Taut: Internet power has been aggregating, dampening the once widely held hope among "net heads" for emergence of an egalitarian utopia.

2. Eliminating "which" and "that" without changing the meaning.

⟶Slack: Microsoft, which continues to force computer manufacturers to install Internet Explorer on new machines, may soon have a stranglehold on access to the Internet.

⟶Taut: Microsoft, still forcing computer manufacturers to install Internet Explorer on new machines, may soon have a stranglehold on access to the Internet.

⟶Slack: Netscape, which won the Internet browser championship title by simply being there first, is being overtaken by Microsoft, a company that can afford to give its browser away because it's the biggest player on the block.

⟶Taut: Because Microsoft is the biggest player on the block, it can afford to give its browser away and take away the Internet browser championship title Netscape earned by simply being there first.

3. Omitting superfluous words and phrases

⟶Slack: It is safe to assume that difficult passages need some trimming and some tightening.

⟶Taut: Assume difficult passages need trimming and tightening.

4. Replace wimpy verbs with strong verbs.

—Slack: Our reading ability is being destroyed by overindulgence in the viewing of television.

—Taut: Excessive television viewing is destroying our ability to read.

—Slack: After much persuasion, the editorial staff could see merit in her ideas.

—Taut: After much persuasion, the editorial staff saw merit in her ideas.

—Slack: A resting period is necessary between revisions.

—Taut: Rest between revisions.

—Slack: I underwent a period of apprenticeship.

—Taut: I apprenticed.

5. Pruning prepositions.

—Slack: The editorial assistant just below the editor was responsible for judging the quality of the manuscripts and was over the other assistants, who were in charge of the sorting of the mail.

—Taut: The immediate assistant to the editor judged the quality of manuscripts and managed the other assistants, who sorted mail.

6. Contracting two or more sentences into one by preceding an explanation or an illustration with a colon, implying "as follows" or "as stated hereafter."

✑ Slack: Microsoft will soon monopolize the software side
of computing. This includes three major areas. One is the
computer operating system. The second is the desktop
office suite. The Internet browser is the third.

✑ Taut: Microsoft will soon monopolize the software side
of computing: the computer operating system, the
desktop office suite, and the Internet browser.

I'm sure this list doesn't cover every possibility, but I'm certain of one
thing: Applying it to your next bit of nonfiction writing will help you to
ward off word flab. And, unlike those diet plans that promise but don't
deliver, this one gets you instant results.

Explaining Too Much: Why More Is Less

by Caro Clarke

*O*ne of the usual mistakes beginners make is to explain too much. How much is too much? Deciding this requires a dispassionate mind, a sense of pace, and a good feeling for what is really necessary for the story. These come with experience, but a beginner can start to develop them by recognizing the cause of explaining too much.

That cause is love. You love your story. You love your characters. You love the world you've invented. You want your readers to see them, appreciate them, and understand them just as you do yourself. And since you don't want your readers to start with the wrong impression, you pile up descriptive scenes as soon as the story opens. Or, if you've read your "how-to-write" manuals (as you ought!), you drop in a big lump of description right after that "grabber" first line you know you're supposed to have.

For instance:

> The car plunged through the barrier and over the cliff.
> Nadine prayed the airbag would save her, her generous mouth opened in a scream, her periwinkle blue eyes fixed in horror on the ocean below, her auburn hair, thick and luxuriant, streaming behind her, her long elegant legs braced for the crash.

Nadine had always been strikingly beautiful, even as a child. Her hair, less golden then, was always held back by a blue ribbon. In summer a few delicious freckles dusted her nose. Wide shoulders had led, in adolescence, to a bosom of graceful proportions. Her hands were elegant, and beauticians often commented on her healthy nails, nails that were now digging into the car's upholstery...

and so on.

How to guard against the mistake of explaining too much? Rewrite your work, excluding every scrap of description. Now how does the story read? If a detail was not necessary, its absence will not be noticed. If you take out all the description from the Nadine section above, you would have a better story (it couldn't be worse).

Personal appearance matters only when it influences a character's motivation or has an impact upon the story. If your protagonist thinks that her big nose makes her ugly and unlovable, she won't believe it when the boy next door says he's crazy about her. If a character plunges into a burning house to rescue a child, it is important that we already know he is disabled. It is not important that he has red hair. You'll be surprised how little description you actually need.

Then there is the problem of the lovingly described setting:

Nobody came to the farmhouse anymore. It was a big square building approached by a long track. Built in the 1890s, when the valley had been opened up by pioneers, the house had a porch on three sides, gable windows, and gingerbread that once had been pristine, but now was gaping here and there like teeth gone bad. The front door barely hung on its hinges and the front hall was full of little tumbleweeds that had trapped themselves and now rolled like dustballs over the rotting hall carpet. The parlor, once the pride of the house, was musty with the smell of decaying horsehair furniture, of wood and fabric neglected. Across the hall, the sitting room...

and so on and so on, through every room of the house.

Where description is necessary, avoid a dull block of descriptive prose by integrating description with action or by having the description filtered through the eyes of a character. The abandoned farmhouse should not be described in advance of its first visitor for ten years, but rather should be seen through the eyes of that visitor. Give the reader the fewest descriptive words necessary to convey the scene. Better to have one piercing sentence than three paragraphs of room-by-room description:

> Harold stopped in the middle of the hall, breathing decay. He could hear the curtains blowing in every room. It was like standing inside an empty heart, desolate, familiar.

The emptiness of the house and the reason Harold is in it begin to come together. Later, you can add a scene, perhaps where he pushes the tumbleweeds out the front door or rubs the dirt off a faded photograph, to build both the atmosphere of a house long neglected and Harold's own personality.

More insidious is the psychological or background description, for this is often considered good writing:

> Daniel came from a long line of copers. He had coped when his father had died, supporting his mother financially and emotionally; he had coped with his wife's illness and miscarriage; and now, facing her across the table, he put on his usual smile as he sorted through the divorce papers. He never questioned why he had carried the burdens or made light of his own feelings. It had always been his duty; he had done it for so long that it felt a part of him.

This might sound fine, but it is actually an info dump. What are you going to say next? How can the conversation do anything but repeat some of this information? Info dumps are never as compelling as action, and dialogue is the most compelling action of all:

> "What's this, honey?" Daniel asked, even though he could see the word "divorce" on the top paper.
> "Don't give me that smile," Joan snapped. "For God's sake, Dan, your life is falling apart."

"Getting angry doesn't solve anything," said Daniel, pressing a blanket of calmness over his feelings. "We can sort this out."

"No, Dan, we can't." Joan sighed. "Sometimes things just can't be sorted out. Especially this. You keep doing what you did with your mother after your father died, but I'm not your mother. I need more from you. Needed more."

Why was she doing this to him? "Honey, I've done the best I knew how." As always.

By revealing the past within present action, you can let it resonate with what is going on now, allowing one to enhance the other. You also avoid boring the reader by preventing the characters from becoming wind-up toys, doing what we have been told they do. It is better to see Daniel "coping" when he is really doing it—or thinks he is.

A basic rule of writing is to have only what propels the narrative, either because it furthers the action or because it illuminates character within that action. Two people rushing through the night to the hospital is action; two people arguing in the car as they rush to the hospital is character development within action. The fact that one of them is six feet tall with blue eyes is neither action nor illumination.

Advice for beginners? Cut. And keep cutting until you think you have reduced your story to a skeleton. The skeleton *is* your story. The rest is blubber.

Characterization

Description

One test of a writer's skill is how she peoples her fictional world.

A, B And C List Characters: To Each According To His Needs, From Each According To Her Necessity

by Caro Clarke

"One more thing: if you upstage me again tonight, I swear to God I'll walk off and leave you standing."

Christine listened to her own voice, professional assessment balancing, but not leavening, her rage.

"That's not fair! I'd never do that." Sam fuelled himself with his hurt. "It's not like you've never hogged my spotlight, and knew you could get away with it. And knew I'd let you!"

The taxi driver turned his head as if movement could crack the icy silence. "You wanna be dropped off at the stage door, Ma'am?"

"Naturally," said Sam, making Christine instantly decree, "The front."

"You're planning, after all, my dear, to make an Entrance?" Horace asked gently from the jumpseat.

"Against your advice?" she snapped. How like him to needle her in front of Sam! With his pseudo-plummy aplomb (oh, that was clever, she must remember that), his silk ascot, and his English leather shoes, he was more theatrical than she would ever deign to be.

"As you pay me 25 percent for it, my dear, why not, just this once, accept it?" he replied.

You pay him 25 percent?" Sam asked, all hurt forgotten for business. "What makes you worth it, Horace?"

The agent eyed Sam's tie. "Because you shall be following Christine into the theater, dear boy, and not vice versa."

"Here y'go," said the driver thankfully, pulling up.

If your story were a movie, the protagonists would be your stars. You would also have supporting actors and walk-ons. In a written story, these are your "A," "B," and "C" characters. In the scene above, Christine and Sam are "A" characters; Horace, the agent, a "B" character, and the unnamed taxi driver a "C."

Your "A" characters *are* your story. The reader has to be able to see them inside and out, either through their self-revelation (their interior dialogue or self-awareness) or through their speech and actions (how they reveal or betray themselves). "A" characters need all your creative power: you have to pour into them all your understanding of human nature, all your eye for detail, in order to make them come alive. And they *must* come alive or your story is dead on the page.

"B" characters assist you and the "A" characters to achieve that living, compelling story. "B" characters, while fully complex and realized, merely support the story, illuminating situations and encouraging—or forcing—the "A" characters to reveal themselves. Horace, by saying things Christine and Sam will react to, helps you tell the reader more about them. But the story is not his story. You don't need to put as much work into getting into his skin. Your main tasks with "B" characters such as Horace are, first, to make them living individuals, not stereotypes and, second, to make sure that they are doing the job they are there to do.

"C" characters are in the story because your world should be filled with people whom your "A" and "B" characters would naturally encounter, such as waitresses, police officers, and taxi drivers. "C" characters, while not brought alive to the same extent as "B" characters, should never be cardboard flats. They should simply be the people there isn't time to learn about in this particular story. The taxi driver in the scene above, for instance, should have the potential of becoming the "A" character in his own story. We should be able to imagine him blowing off stream to his wife: "You'll never guess who I had in the back today, and, boy, was it a ride from hell!" The scene you've written happens not to be his story, just as it is not Horace's story. There is no point in fleshing either character out if this does not advance the telling of Christine and Sam's story. You need from your "C" and "B" characters only what helps you propel the narrative, and nothing more. It is Christine and Sam who need everything you've got.

One test of a writer's skill is how she peoples her fictional world. A fully realized "A" character will not be found living among stereotypes or nonentities, just as properly created "B" and "C" characters will not be so distractingly interesting as to overshadow the "A" characters. All should have their places. It is your job to give them what they need so that they can give the story what it needs.

> Horace stepped from the taxi into the babbling crowd, murmuring, "Ah, how they love her." He held the door for Christine, whose heart leaped as she immersed herself in her fans. How she loved them! Everything forgiven within this flood of adoration, she smiled at Sam.
>
> He smiled in return. One day they would love him as much. Maybe more.

Do Your Characters Have Emotions? How Do We Know?

by Tricia Bush

When you watch a movie or a television program, if the acting is any good at all, you know what the characters are feeling. All you have to do is watch. To suggest emotion with facial expression is relatively easy. Conveying emotions in writing, however, is not. Many writers try to fudge by simply stating, "he was angry," "confused," "bored," "happy," etc. In other words, they merely tell us what the characters are feeling. This is cheating, and readers know it.

Take, for example, the movie *Braveheart*. How would you, as a writer, convey the emotions on Mel Gibson's face as he turns from the grave of the woman he loved? "He is sad"? Come on, you can do better than that. How about the expression on his face when he turns to face her father? "He looks guilty"? What a writer must do is convey the guilt, anguish, and naked pain that Gibson shows physically, in words that conjure an image equally as moving as the one in the movie. Why bother? You can watch the movie. True. But think of this: if you can learn to capture such emotions in a meaningful and imaginative way, you are well on your way to becoming a professional writer. That kind of art is worth doing, and worth doing well.

Making emotions come alive on the page takes some thought. You could write for the *Braveheart* scene, "The grief and guilt he felt showed plainly on his face." Well, okay. But compare that with the following: "He knelt beside the cold, wet grave. Her face, seen dimly through the shroud, was peaceful, as after love. When he stood up from that place, his naked soul was in his eyes. He looked at her father and knelt before him, mute and beseeching, and bowed his head as if to say, do what thou wilt. Wordless, he received the blessing hand that trembled as it touched his damp hair; wordless, he would have received a killing thrust. The pain remained in his eyes as he rose, but he could stand now, and he could fight."

Whew! Nope, that ain't easy. The prose may not be great, but it certainly wasn't easy.

Emotions, rendered convincingly, add richness to every aspect of a written work. They make characters deeper and more sympathetic, they provide motivation that moves plot, they permeate the work with authenticity.

In a manuscript I once read, the main character is a woman in her seventies. She muses that cloth sewn with bitterness cannot be redesigned into something else, that the bitterness remains. Later, she reinforces how she feels by likening her surface "good manners" to the gooey honey she uses to sweeten her tea.

What has she shown us? That she is bitter, that she has tried not to be, and has failed. That bitterness is like cloth or the acrid bite of unsweetened tea; it is what it is no matter what you do with it. That's what these passages say to me. They may say something else to you. No matter—if they speak to you at all about the character, you are in the process of making her your own.

Nearly all emotions are compound. Rarely is an emotion felt that doesn't have a trace of one or more other feelings mixed in. You might think you are feeling pure anger, but that anger is probably mixed with anxiety, confusion, sadness, guilt, and/or fear. Emotions are complex, and conveying them is a complex process. As an exercise I sometimes do what I did above with that wordless scene from *Braveheart*: try to convey what the movie or television characters are feeling, given the expressions on their faces.

Emotions also vary in intensity. If you look in a thesaurus under the emotion you wish to convey, the entries will give you ideas about the degree of emotion you want. I've just looked up "fear," for example, and found entries that range from "dismay" and "nervousness" to "panic" and "terror." To say "He was afraid" robs the reader of a valuable insight in to the character's feelings. "He was uneasy" does not mean what "He was terrified" does. Yet both of these would fall under the "He was afraid" umbrella. Pinpointing the degree of emotion enriches a character and can help generate dialogue and action. An uneasy character will speak and act differently from one who is terrified.

Emotions also have ages. Temper tantrums, for example, suggest childishness or perhaps arrested development. Bitterness, on the other hand, is an old emotion. No one becomes bitter in a moment—it takes longer than that. Bitterness is the result of many negative emotions, brooded over and held close over a period of time.

Conveying emotions well brings a depth and a richness to writing that make the reader feel what you want him to feel about the character and about the story you are telling. Attention to this aspect of character development will make your work fuller, more complete, more interesting, and more memorable.

Finding And Building
The Spine Of Your Story

by Eileen Alcorn Workman

*I*n December, many of us set out on a competitive and exhausting search to locate the biggest, straightest tree we can possibly find. We opt for a tree because its very treeness projects a symmetry—a centeredness—that is at once majestic and beautiful. The branches, anchored as they are to the trunk, are strong enough to bear the weight of our ornaments but not so thick as to bury them in foliage, and the narrowing top provides the focal point we need for the star, its crowning glory.

So it should be with a well-crafted novel. If we toss lovely prose and interesting characters into a bushy, purposeless story, what we end up with are a lot of pretty but messy vignette clumps that leave a reader with no sense of unity. A tale with spine, on the other hand, gives a reader a strong sense of connectedness to the core of our story.

A wonderful example of a tale with a well-crafted spine is Margaret Mitchell's *Gone With The Wind*. Scarlett O'Hara, the novel's main character, has a problem: the war has threatened to destroy that which she holds most dear, her family plantation, Tara. From the moment Scarlett first recognizes her love for the land, every choice she makes and every problem or obstacle she faces stems from her obsession to rescue Tara from disaster. As a result, despite the epic and sweeping nature of Mitchell's tale, the reader never loses sight of the central focus of the story, Scarlett's desire to preserve and protect her beloved Tara.

How does a writer go about finding the center of his story? The simplest way is to ask the question "Who is my main character and what is his or her problem?" If you can't answer that question in one brief sentence, you haven't yet discovered the spine of your story. This needn't be cause for panic; some writers choose to write on until the center reveals itself, while others prefer to sit back and ponder what they've already written, then outline the future story until they've forged a solid framework upon which to build. Whatever your personal method, keep asking yourself the who-and-what question—daily or hourly if need be—until you are able to answer it both honestly and briskly.

Once you have a handle on your story's spine, the next step is to begin to tailor your novel so that your story builds inexorably toward a climax. This means gritting your teeth and pruning away the pretty prose that leads a reader away from your unifying problem. To illustrate, let's go back to our Christmas tree for a moment. At times, a number of perfectly healthy but low-hanging branches must be cut away from the tree's base to keep them from dragging, while in other places branches may need to be tied up to fill in the bare spots. So should your unproductive story elements be trimmed and your bare spots filled in as you create a perfect balance between prose and story.

When choosing which elements to cut, consider two questions to test the strength of your material. First, is your protagonist bound to the central problem, and is he or she the character who must solve it? If not, you'd be well served to rethink either your main character or your main problem because the energy in your story will fall flat if your problem and your protagonist are not inexorably connected. Second, ask yourself if each specific situation, complication, or obstacle you've created somehow relates to the main character and that character's attempts to solve the problem. If not, I challenge you to question your motives for including that story segment. This is where the phrase "killing your darlings" comes from; it takes a disciplined professional to fight the urge to leave in scenes that are wonderfully written but have nothing to do with furthering the underlying story.

Once you've pruned your story effectively, it will become obvious that certain elements have been underwritten and need developing to balance the action. To test your writing in these areas, ask yourself whether your main character is making active choices along the way. If not—if the action is happening to him instead of emanating from him—you will find you're left with a weak and listless story. To strengthen it, seek new ways to deepen your protagonist's commitment to solving his problem, then increase his number of choices and obstacles along the way. The greater the consequences of his ultimate failure, the closer the sympathetic bond between reader and character.

In simpler terms, seek new ways to raise your story's stakes. A life or death struggle has far more impact than leaving a reader wondering whether your hero will or won't get that *A* in history class. Unless of course, the failure to get an *A* means failure to get into college, which means failure to inherit the family business, which leads to failure to win the woman he loves, which leads to ultimate depression and suicide...you get the picture.

Another good way to enrich your story is to focus on your character's vulnerability. The more *at risk* your protagonist appears, the more your reader will connect with him, no matter how flawed he may seem on the surface. What I'm suggesting here is that you give your readers a private peek into your protagonist's soul, then help them to like what they see. Give them something—and someone—to root for as the story progresses. By building on your main character's altruism and selflessness (i.e., his goals are noble and his motives are genuine) and by giving him a high-stakes problem to solve, you will create a strong, straight story spine. Stay focused on it to the end, and your reader can't help connecting deeply with your story.

Writing "Bad": How To Create A Memorable Villain

by Sunnye Tiedemann

"You must pay the rent."

"I can't pay the rent."

"I'll pay the rent."

Those lines from an old melodrama define three essential characters: the villain, the victim, and the hero. But if you're writing a mystery for publication in today's market, simple stereotypes just won't do.

"The mystery novel is a game between author and reader, the goal of which is to find the villain," writes Shannon O'Cork in *How To Write Mysteries*.

So how do you create a villain?

Very carefully.

You've already determined when and where the tale begins and which character is central to the story—our protagonist—and you've selected the victim and the villain.

Now, learn all there is to know about your Bad Guy. He (or she –"he" will be used to prevent pronoun proliferation) started life as everyone does, a sweet, innocent babe. What went wrong?

A good place to begin is with motive: why does he kill or steal or...whatever? The answer to that leads to the question of how. And why does the protagonist care? One question leads to another until you know all about this character's past and present and how they intertwine with those of your protagonist and victim.

There are a few important points to keep in mind as you work. In contemporary mystery fiction, you stand the best chance of being published if your villain, or antagonist:

— is an interesting, vital person who at first seems perfectly normal. But he is maniacally driven to win. He will do everything in his considerable power to accomplish his goal and to keep from getting caught.

— has a character flaw that leads to his undoing. Eve Sandstrom (*Death Down Home, The Devil Down Home* and *The Violence Beat* Worldwide Press) observes how a personality gone wrong can pique a reader's interest: "I've always been fascinated by why good people do bad things...[W]e see the phenomenon often in cases of public employees, for instance. This 'good goes bad' situation interests me. It's something that could happen to any of us."

— has an excellent reason for his actions that is clearly presented to the reader. "I don't like the old cliche that he [the villain] should be nice to his dog even if he tortures and kills. But the reader ought to at least understand why he behaves as he does," says Meg Chittenden, author of the Charlie Plato mystery series and *How To Write Your Novel* (Kensington).

— has a goal. It may be as simple as not getting caught, but he must have something to strive for.

— is involved in the victim's life or at least is on the periphery so that suspicion will naturally fall on him.

— will have a substantial and effective role in the story. It pays to map out his role—his own private plot—putting him in continual opposition to the protagonist.

~ is clever and is able to take advantage of circumstances and use them to his advantage such that finding him will be a challenge for the protagonist. Remember, the effective villain will not be ruthless in everything. He will act like a normal human being most of the time.

In *Techniques Of The Selling Writer*, Dwight Swain writes, "*Role-wise*, the strength of your villain is the strength of your story." The Bad Guy personifies threat and evil in the story, and, by doing so, gives the story unity. He also sets up a perfect catch 22 to keep the story moving: The protagonist attempts to thwart the villain or to find him; the villain reacts and intensifies the drama.

It is by facing the adversity caused by the villain that the protagonist demonstrates he deserves to win. The tougher the challenges he faces, the more resourceful the hero must be. Severe adversity makes the final triumph a moment of supreme satisfaction for the reader.

There are two schools of thought, each valid, concerning the degree of evil that is necessary for creating an effective villain. "An antagonist shouldn't be all evil," says Chittenden in a private interview. "It seems to me, much more effective to have the villain who appears quite attractive and behaves fairly well most of the time, but is twisted inside."

On the other hand, William Diehl, author of best-sellers *Primal Fear* (Villard), *Show Of Evil*, and *Reign In Hell* (Ballantine), created Aaron Stampler, one of the most horrifying villains in contemporary literature.

"I initially started with two characters: [Martin] Vail and Naomi Chance," he says in a private interview. "The spine of the story was to be a sharp, arrogant, unbearable lawyer who outwits himself ... [and] Aaron Stampler started in my mind as a sympathetic character. I created a case which seemed impossible to win. I wanted to believe in Stampler's innocence and then I decided on the multiple personality disorder switch....Then I got to the last line of the book...[and] with that one line, Stampler becomes an arch villain, although most readers are sympathetic right to the last line, as was I. Now the reader thinks about it and replays the book in his/her mind, which is always a strong way to finish a novel."

In earlier books, Diehl used more conventional methods to create villains. An example is *27*—reissued and retitled *The Hunt* (Ballantine) in 1996. "I created Siebenzwanzig (Nazi actor turned spy) before I created Keegan, the hero," Diehl says. "The actor is shown as an intense Nazi and a psychopath....I show why he is that way...a man to be reckoned with...a man who really enjoys killing. In both cases we understand why these men are evil incarnate."

Barbara Paul (*Full Frontal Murder*, Scribner, and *Fare Play*, Worldwide) sums it up nicely. "Always keep in mind that an antagonist does what he does because he is convinced it's the best thing for him to do. No matter how warped his reason sounds, to him it makes sense. No matter how much a villain's reason may reek of excuse-making, it's still the principle upon which he acts and that principle must be clear and convincing if you are to avoid creating a cartoonish villain—a guy who is a bad guy only because you need a bad guy in your story."

O'Cork, Shannon. *How To Write Mysteries*. Writers Digest Books, 1989, ASIN: 0898793726

Chittenden, Meg. *How To Write Your Novel*. Writer, 1995, ISBN: 0871161788

Swain, Dwight. *Techniques Of The Selling Writer*. University of Oklahoma Press, 1982, ISBN: 0806111917

What color dominates your character's world, or has a special meaning to her?

It's Not Easy Bein' Green: Using Color In Your Writing

by Karen L. Oberst

eing aware of what colors mean to characters can make stories richer and stronger. You can use color to add authenticity to your writing in at least two ways: by using more precise wording when you refer to a color, and by being aware of the connotations attached to various colors. This article focuses on green, the most common color in nature.

In a sixty-four Crayola™ Crayon box, there are: forest green, pine green, olive green, sea green, aquamarine, blue-green, yellow-green, green-yellow, and spring green.

Outside the crayon box, we have: kelly green, chartreuse, pea green, mint green, celery, hunter green, lime, turquoise, emerald green, jade green, gray green, avocado, sea foam, teal, aqua, and more. Each is a slightly different shade and will bring a different picture to your reader's mind. Kelly green might bring memories of St. Patrick's Day; emerald green, of expensive jewelry; gray green, of the leaves of olive trees; avocado, of the seventies (when it was used so frequently in home decoration); turquoise, of southwestern jewelry, and so on.

Green can be described by its relation to other things. In *The Fellowship Of The Ring*, J. R. R. Tolkien writes that Goldberry is wearing a dress as "green as young reeds." C. S. Lewis, in *The Silver Chair*, describes a snake being "as green as poison." In a more popular vein, one might say, "as green as Kermit the Frog."

Psychologists describe green as a restful color. People tend to think of the outdoors when they think of green, of trees, and mountains —places of low stress. On the other hand, it is also the color of putrefaction, of decay and mold.

Indeed, green has many meanings. It may connote fresh and new, as spring green; or indicate growth and life, as a green thumb; or as in Psalm 92:14, "They will still bear fruit in old age, they will stay fresh and green." It can mean untried, as a green boy; or immature in the sense of not ripe, as green apples. It is slang for money. It can mean jealousy, as the green-eyed monster. It can indicate readiness to go, as a green light, or a space launch being "condition green." You can play on the greens at a golf course. It can even indicate that you are part of the environmental movement.

What color dominates your character's world, or has a special meaning to her? What connotations does that color have for her? By answering these questions, you may have a richer story to tell.

Tolkien, J.R.R. *The Fellowship Of The Ring*. Houghton Mifflin, 1988 (Reissue), ASIN: 0395272238

Lewis, C.S. *The Silver Chair*. Harpercollins Juvenile Books, 1994 (Reprint), ISBN: 0020444206

Character Goals

*The minute you have an even number of
anything, pairs are formed, and the work
becomes still, static, and very likely boring.*

The Golden Triangle:
Characters In Threes

By Tricia Bush

Many writers are also painters or musicians or practitioners of another art in addition to writing. I was a painter long before I started to write seriously, and I have noticed some formal similarities between painting and writing.

For centuries, artistic composition has followed a formula developed by Pythagoras, that of the "Golden Triangle." This *triangle* is the place on the canvas, determined by mathematics, where the center in the painting will be most effective. As we are not talking about painting, I will not go into how this position is determined, other than to mention its existence.

There is a *convention* of artistic composition that is called "the rule of three," which simply means that, if you are going to have similar elements (such as trees) in your painting, you should place at least three trees, rather than two, on the canvas. This rule has to do with balance. If you have two trees, one on either side of the canvas, you achieve a kind of static balance; when you add a third tree, you add it closer to one of the trees than to the other. This creates more weight on one side and therefore more interest, than do two equal trees in balance. Specifically, the imbalance creates *tension*. Even numbers of objects tend to *pair* with each other, with each pair having equal importance, and that equilibrium makes for a composition without movement.

Try the following even if you don't have any desire to draw or paint. Doodle a tree on the left side of a piece of paper, and then draw an identical tree on the right side of the paper. Look at it. Then draw a third, smaller tree, somewhere near one of the two original trees. Do you see what happens? Now put your finger or a piece of paper over the third tree. Can you see that the addition of that third tree provides a sort of movement that was not there before? Or, take a seesaw with two equally weighted children on either end of the center support, the fulcrum. Unless some other force comes into play, they will merely sit there, perfectly balanced, forever. Add a little more weight to one end, and suddenly the two sides have to do something to attain that balance. This is "action." The "rule of three" can be extrapolated into a general rule, and that is this: always use an odd number of "trees" in your composition (whether or not they are trees). The minute you have an even number of anything, pairs are formed, and the work becomes still, static, and very likely boring.

How does this rule apply to writing? Imperfectly, to be sure. Many short stories feature only two major characters. This pairing is a function of length. In a short story, there is neither the space nor the need for in-depth character development. Many short stories feature only limited reciprocal action: A relates to B, and B relates to A.

The two major characters typically needed in longer fiction are a protagonist and an antagonist. Here we have two opposing forces. The usual convention is to have the protagonist just a tiny bit stronger than the antagonist but in ways that are not readily apparent at the beginning of a story. Since we do not initially know (ideally, or there would be no *tension*), that the protagonist is *heavier* than the antagonist, this sets up as a static situation: two equal but opposite forces contending with each other for some goal.

But now add a third *force*, or character. Immediately, the situation becomes dynamic. The third element will sometimes have more importance, sometimes less, but the added element (whether a force of nature, an inner conflict, or another character) adds depth and movement to the plot. Character A (the protagonist) must relate both to character B (the antagonist) and element/character C. Character B must relate to both A and C, and C must relate to A and B.

In his excellent book *Theme and Strategy*, Ronald B. Tobias states that (other than in the case of short stories) "the most common character dynamic has three major characters." He goes on to say that, with the addition of the third character, the dynamic changes from a factor of two to a factor of six. This creates a triangle.

Imagine an argument about divorce between two people. They shout back and forth. For a while this can be interesting, but the longer it goes on, the more boring it becomes. Suppose their child enters during the argument. Suddenly, it is not a tug-of-war between two characters—we now have a triad in which both of the two arguing characters must relate to the third character, the child. Many plot patterns depend on the triangle, without which there would be no plot. The obvious ones that come to mind are those involving adultery or rivalry.

But what about novels that contain many characters who interact in some significant way with the primary three characters? If three major characters are good, wouldn't four major characters be better? No, for the reason that the dynamic factor then reaches twelve. Twelve important relationships among four characters are nearly impossible to keep track of at the same time.

So what does a writer do when he wants to add more characters to his novel, ones who are important but are not the main characters around which the plot revolves? In most cases, these characters form triangles of their own, with the major triad characters interacting with them at various points in the story.

Tobias states, "The important rule to remember when developing triangles in your work is that the triangles should not compete with each other. Develop them in a hierarchy of importance. The major characters have their triangle; the minor characters have theirs. One major character, such as the central character of your work, may participate in more than one triangle, but you should avoid confusing the reader with too many relationships, especially if they are of equal importance." In other words, one of the major characters might form the third point of a triangle briefly, but this association is weaker than the primary triangle association.

Taking the example of Shakespeare, Tobias points out that the Bard "often limited his triangles to three: one major and two minors, and according to 'the rule of three,' that is the perfect balance."

This statement made me curious, so I got out my copy of Shakespeare's plays to test its validity. I did not, of course, have the time to read and analyze all of the plays of Shakespeare, but, concentrating on the tragedies, I found at least two triads in most of them. Actually the pattern seems to be a major triangle, a minor triangle, and another that is still more distant from the main triad. In Hamlet, for example, the major triangle is composed of Hamlet, Claudius, and Hamlet's mother. The second triangle is composed of Ophelia, Laertes, and Polonius. The third triangle is composed of Horatio, Rosencrantz, and Guildenstern (one faithful and two unfaithful "friends" of Hamlet's from Wittenberg).

The "minor" triangles are marvelous for subplots. In The Fiction Writer's Silent Partner, Martin Roth observes, "A subplot is a secondary story linked to the master plot, or it may be on its own, not directly involved in the master plot but affecting one or more of the principle characters." For example, to paraphrase Roth, in a mystery, the main plot is to discover the murderer. Suppose that, at the same time, one of the detectives assigned to the case is having domestic problems, or has a child who is in difficulties or is ill. These relational points will have an effect on the detective's emotions (and possibly his actions), but they have no bearing on the main plot, which is to find the murderer. This is an example of an unconnected subplot. A connected subplot would be one in which one of the detectives falls in love, and the love interest turns out to have information that leads to the detection of the murderer.

Patricia D. Cornwell's series character, Kay Scarpetta, is the protagonist in her mysteries. As the chief medical examiner for the Commonwealth of Virginia, she is always central. The murderer is the antagonist. But Kay has other relationships. She has a relationship with a police sergeant named Marino. Since they work the cases together, the relationship between them affects Kay's words and actions as well as Marino's words and actions. This, then, is the typical main triad of a Patricia Cornwell mystery: Scarpetta, Marino, and the murderer. A secondary regular triad in Kay's world is made up of her mother, her sister, and her sister's daughter, Lucy. The plots are enriched with glimpses of Kay's affection for her niece, her exasperation with her sister, and her relationship with her mother—none of which is essential to the main plot, but without which her character would be less complex and less interesting.

When a friend of mine heard what I was using as my subject for this article, she said, "My first novel had only two characters, and I couldn't understand why it wasn't 'flowing' as smoothly as I thought it should. But when I added that third character, it began writing itself. It not only flowed, it grew wings and soared."

I cannot guarantee that adding a third primary character, or a secondary triad, or a series of triads that impinge upon each other in different ways will be the magic key to unlock the golden door, but if you find yourself blocked, try adding a third something somewhere. It may be just the element you were looking for.

Tobias, Ronald B. *Theme and Strategy*, Writer's Digest Books, 1989, ISBN 0-89879-392-0

Roth, Martin. *The Fiction Writer's Silent Partner*, Writer's Digest Books, 1991, ISBN 0-89879-482-X

What an author reveals
and what he or she conceals
determine our responses.

The Character Of Characters

by Laura Bagby

T here are several ways a reader comes to know and understand a character: through what the character says, what the character does, what other characters say about the character, and what the narrator tells us. In nineteenth-century fiction, the narrator often spoke directly about a character, but that device has gone out of style in favor of letting the reader discern the character's nature. The narrator still influences the way we see a character, however, by telling us things that may make us better understand the character's behavior. This is also true when the character himself is the narrator.

Practiced writers know that a sympathetic character does not have to be perfect. In fact, characters who are too rich, too beautiful, and too wonderful may fail to please because readers themselves have flaws and can relate better to characters who also have idiosyncrasies and character defects. The writer manipulates us into a reaction to a character.

> He leaned over the half-empty dishes and said, "Money doesn't mean anything to me. People always matter more than money."
>
> "My ex-husband doesn't think so," she said. The exotic salmon and shrimp were grumbling in her stomach like jet-setters in a Greyhound. She drank a little more champagne from her nearly empty glass, hoping it would settle things down before she ejected the alien cuisine onto the white linen tablecloth.

She excused herself to go to the powder room. As she turned the corner in the lobby, she heard their waiter say, "The old fool—a hundred dollar meal! And I'll bet he'll leave the usual dollar tip!" This comment was followed by laughter. She could sympathize since she had waited tables right after her divorce ten years ago. She, too, had known all the stingy tippers who were regular customers.

She arrived back at the table just as the waiter brought Tom the tray with his change. The waiter set the tray down and with great sincerity wished both of them a good evening. Tom scooped up two dollar bills, leaving one dollar, one dime, one nickel, and four pennies. As he rushed around to help her with her coat, her stomach tightened at the memory of the waiter's remarks that she had overheard.

In the fictional passage above, what do we know about Tom? We know that he thinks he is generous, but that his actions, in this instance, are miserly. We know that the waiter is familiar with, and contemptuous of, Tom's stinginess. And we know that Tom's dinner companion finds his lack of generosity embarrassing. Of course, if we were to read more about Tom, we might encounter conflicting information from other sources. For example, his best friend might describe him as a man with a big heart, and his ex-wife might thank him for continuing to pay her rehab bills. It is the aggregate of this information that helps readers decide whether or not they sympathize with the character.

The writer manipulates our reaction to a character. For example, the narrator can give or withhold information that will influence the way we respond. If, after the above scene, we see Tom slip a twenty-dollar bill to the waiter behind his companion's back, we begin to like him better or at least give him a chance to reveal why he has hidden the tip from his date.

Real people are complex, and so are well-written characters. Complex characterization requires some conflicts in the character's behavior or conflicts in other characters' perceptions. How do you feel about Tom in the scene above? Is he complex? No, he appears to be a stereotype. But suppose that, in addition to slipping the waiter a twenty, he surreptitiously slips the two ones he picked up from the tray to a homeless bag lady they pass in the parking lot? Will you then feel different about him? Would you have to question your assumption that the waiter was talking about the man we thought he was? What if you found out later that Tom owns the restaurant and was playing a standing joke on the waiter, who knew that he'd receive an extra fifty dollars at the end of the week for going along with the joke?

What an author reveals and what he or she conceals determine our responses. Let's look at another scene, presented two different ways. What elements of character revelation affect your reaction to the character?

Scene 1:

Jim walked wearily up the stairs to his one—room apartment. Tonight the stairs seemed endless, but finally he reached the top floor and glanced into the communal hall bathroom. He longed for a shower instead of the old claw-footed bathtub that filled as slowly as a creek bed in the dry season. Jim's young neighbor rushed past him, nearly pushing Jim back down the stairs in his hurry. "Hi, Jim. How's it going?" The boy did not wait for a reply.

Jim turned left and inserted his key in the lock. The door dragged open on the uneven floor. The room seemed close and stale after the spacious restaurant. He kicked off his shoes and folded his tall frame into the single chair. From that angle, his eyes were on a level with the only picture in the room: a young woman smiling mischievously into the camera, or perhaps into the eyes of the amateur photographer, so long ago. As his head dropped to his chest, he could hear her soft voice repeating the words he could never forget. . . .

Scene 2:

Jim walked up the stairs to his apartment. He reached the top floor and glanced into the communal hall bathroom. Even from outside the door, he could see a ring of scum around the huge old tub. His neighbors, he thought as he did every night, were pigs. Just then one of them came scurrying down the hall. Seeing Jim, the boy averted his eyes and rushed past him as though to escape obvious and eminent danger.

Jim turned left and inserted his key into the massive lock. No one knew why he needed such a hefty lock; the neighbors speculated about whether he was trying to keep himself in or someone else out. Jim swung the door in and, in almost the same motion, swung it shut again. He clicked the lock into place with satisfaction. Carefully, he removed his highly polished shoes and set them side by side against the wall. Pulling up his trousers so that they wouldn't crease unnecessarily, he sat upright on the only chair in the room. Directly in his line of vision was a photograph of a woman; her accusing eyes met his. Quickly he dropped his eyes and wondered for the millionth time why he kept the offensive photograph in plain view. It was bad enough that he could hear her pleading voice, repeating words he could never forget. . . .

The difference in description, of course, gives you a sense of the main character in the first scenario that is different from the character in the second scenario. The differing reactions of the neighbor likewise help to differentiate the two Jims. Certainly, the differing actions of the main character suggest two distinct individuals with different histories. Which one did you like better? Which one intrigued you most?

Remember that there are several ways of depicting your characters' personalities, intentions and motivations. A well-written character will be complex, and you can best demonstrate that complexity by using all the character development techniques available. It is your *job* as the writer to manipulate your readers' responses to your characters.

Finding The Right Names For Your Characters

by John Moir

*M*ost books on writing fiction advise writers to get to know their characters thoroughly. Often, these books suggest creating a profile or backstory to help a writer "learn" enough to make characters interesting and believable.

But along with a personal history, each character requires a name. Finding the right name, I have discovered, can be a bedeviling task. As many times as I have constructed characters in my work, it still seems to take me longer than it should to come up with the perfect name for one of my creations.

It's okay to pull a character's hair color out of thin air. But names really matter, which is why so much rumination seems to be required. A name is often the first piece of information we divulge about a character, and it can give the reader both obvious and subtle clues about who the person is. Names can reveal gender, social class, ethnic background, age, and even personality characteristics.

What makes name selection tricky is that a character name is like other fictional elements: It has to appear believable while operating under constraints not found in real life.

These constraints include the following:

> ➤ Character names must not be too ordinary. For example, a writer had better have a good reason for calling a protagonist "John Smith." Otherwise, this very common name will jar the reader and imply that the writer was too lazy to come up with a "real" name.

> ➤ Fictional names must not be too complicated, either. Very long names or ones that are difficult to pronounce are not good choices—my own last name, Moir (pronounced "Moyer")—would be a poor choice.

> ➤ Fictional names need to complement one another. In real life, two cousins may both be named Mike; in fiction, this would be confusing to the reader. One of those Mikes should be called something else. Even characters with names that start with the same letter who appear together in the same scene are a potential problem. For example, "Donna" and "Debra" are harder for the reader to keep straight than "Donna" and "Katie."

> ➤ Some names are, in effect, already taken. Names with a strong identification such as "Oprah," "Rocky," or "Madonna," are a hard sell to the reader.

So how does a writer go about finding the right name for a character? Sometimes, the name simply emerges along with the rest of the character's attributes. More often, writers need help.

A few years ago, in order to make this process easier, I went to a used bookstore and bought several "name your baby" books. I use them as a thesaurus to select the right name. My favorite is called *The Heroes and Heroines Baby Name Book* by Nancy Heffernan and Louis Judson. It not only gives hundreds of choices but provides background on each one that can help you find a match with the character personality you have in mind.

The book is also helpful in naming different-aged characters since names go in and out of fashion. For example, the name "Ethel" is fine for an older character but a poor fit for a teenager. The book's section on the most popular names of different decades gives writers many good choices.

Names have other subtleties. Certain names tend to distinguish social class. A carpenter can be named Joe while Joseph works better for a college professor. Some names are strong (Samson), wise (Solomon), or dorky (Gilligan). As in real life, it's the personality behind the name that matters, but aligning a character's name with his or her personality helps the reader.

Although last names are sometimes less important and may not even be used for all characters, finding the right one is important. For that, I use the telephone book or other directory, paging through it at random until I find a name that seems right.

I have to confess that I often put off naming a character right away, hoping the right moniker will jump out at me as I work with the story. Maybe this is just procrastination, but I do think the better defined a character is, the better the name you can give him or her. Sometimes I type in "XXX" or some other place holder until either a name comes to me or I grit my teeth and break out the books to do research.

Once I have chosen a name, the next step is to test it by reading my work to my writer's group. Sometimes what I thought was a great name presents a problem I didn't see. Occasionally, the group makes suggestions, (an oh-so-excellent method of name selection: let someone else do it.)

Reading other writers to see how they handle character names is also helpful. Stephen King, for example, who often uses dozens of characters in a book, does an excellent job of selecting names that fit his characters.

No doubt there are successful novelists who choose names carelessly without considering what I have suggested here. Nevertheless, because the right name sharpens and defines a character, it's worth the time and thought to get it right.

Heffernan, Nancy and Judson, Louis. *The Heroes and Heroines Baby Name Book.* Prima Publishing, 1990, ASIN: 155958033X

Writers And Writing

Workshops/ Groups/ Conferences

What To Take To A Writers' Conference
(And What To Do When You Get There)

by Sunnye Tiedemann

S o you've selected the conference that best suits your needs and you're beginning to get excited. You've made your reservations and travel arrangements, and now it's time to pack. So, what do you take to a writer's conference? As a veteran of several, each of which has resulted in either sales or some other advancement in my career, I have some suggestions.

> 1. Pack a positive attitude. No, I'm not kidding. As in most ·
> activities and in life, you'll reap what you sow. Go looking
> for information and ideas, for new friends and contacts, for
> new experiences and attitudes.

At one conference I attended several years ago, we each had a room in a college dorm. My next-door-neighbor was a sweet young lady, but very shy. I never saw her at any of the informal chats. She sat in the back row in a couple of the workshops I attended and affected a bored attitude. She seldom participated in discussions and when she did speak out it was either defensively or in an aggressively challenging manner. I tried several times to include her when opportunities came up to socialize with agents and editors and each time she refused. When the conference was over and we were checking out, she told me she was going to demand her money back. "I've been here for three days and I haven't learned a thing. I haven't met anyone and I didn't get anything out of it," she complained. What did I get? I sold two articles, met an agent, got some ideas for articles from an editor and more from a workshop, and met the publisher of a small publication who asked for a piece. The difference? Our attitudes.

Go expecting to learn and look for opportunities. Meet people. Do things.

2. Dress comfortably. Some conferences are more informal than others, so check with someone to see what's expected. Generally, though, you can't go wrong with a skirt or slacks, a blouse or a shirt, and a sweater with neat and comfortable shoes. You'll probably need at least one dressy outfit for a banquet, and don't forget to take your walking clothes. You'll need exercise after a day of sitting in workshops and panels.

3. Bring your portfolios and manuscripts, but don't expect to have them read by agents or editors unless those arrangements have been made earlier. Why bring them at all? Because you may hit it lucky and casually mention something to someone who might want to see it. Be prepared.

4. A laptop computer is a handy thing to have but a notebook and pen or pencil do just as well. Plan to take notes during sessions and never mind if no one else seems to. Later, you'll be glad you did.

5. Another thing you might use in workshops and sessions is a tape recorder. Even if you see one set up (or especially if you do), ask permission to record. And be ready with extra batteries, just in case. Anticipating your question — yes, I take notes, too.

6. A camera, film, and batteries may not be a must on your list, but they surely can add to the fun. Have your picture

made with your favorite writers; they'll most likely be flattered, and you'll have a treasured souvenir.

7. By all means, bring an alarm clock. Some hotel wake-up services aren't reliable, and the service may not exist on a college campus. This is one time when you could miss something truly important if you're late!

8. Bring a pillow, just in case. Besides, it's nice to have your very own!

When you get there, work the conference. Meet people; introduce yourself; ask questions; talk to authors, editors, and agents about their work. Find someone who's interested in the same things you are; share experiences and ideas. Critique each other's work. Trade notes with people who attended sessions you missed but are curious about. Don't take yourself too seriously; listen and learn.

And don't forget to have a good time!

Eileen's Top Ten Reasons To Attend A Quality Writing Conference

by Eileen Alcorn Workman

1. *To learn humility.* You begin a workshop secure in the knowledge that you're probably the best writer there, the only one with a real chance of critical success. Then you hear other people read their work. And you realize that some of them are wonderful. Better than you. Much better. And still not published. It gives you serious pause.

2. *To learn critical skills.* Learning to critique others is the single most important element in learning to edit yourself. By listening to others' works impartially and learning to determine what is wrong with the structure/content/character development of the pieces, you learn how to apply those same principles to your own work (one hopes with an equal level of detachment).

3. *To get a fresh perspective.* Garnering critique can be bruising, but it can also resurrect a dead or stalled project. Sometimes, a fresh ear and suggestion are all it takes to turn an idea around. This has happened to me at every conference I've attended, whether in casual conversation or in the context of a formal workshop. I'll mention an idea I'm stuck on, and someone will say, "What if you did it *this* way...?" They're usually right.

4. *To network, network, network.* Nothing is quite as satisfying as seeing the name of someone you've commiserated with at a conference on the spine of a hardback novel the following year. I've made more friends, developed more contacts, and established a more amazing network of critique artists these past few years than I'd ever dreamed possible. Networking is also a great way to get the names of agents (good and bad) and to learn which editors are looking for what types of materials.

5. *To develop your craft.* While conferences can't teach you the art of writing or instill you with natural talent, they can and do offer information on the discipline of writing. Learning the craft is just as important as knowing how to create beautiful prose. Seminars on structure, how to create believable dialogue, plot development, the basics of mystery writing, etc. are invaluable to the beginning writer and offer regular refreshment to the advanced writer.

6. *To build your library.* Listen to the titles of books discussed in workshops. Jot down the names of those that have positively influenced the writers you admire. Buy them and read them. Often. They help.

7. *To learn about publishing.* Most conferences will have at least one speaker who discusses the ins and outs of the business side of writing. It's important for writers to understand how and when to acquire an agent, how to submit a professional-looking manuscript, and how to determine the differences between vanity presses, small presses, and commercial presses. Often we get so caught up in the artistic process of writing that we forget we must market what we produce if we ever hope to see it in print.

8. *To experience immersion therapy.* Most beginning writers and many advanced ones have other jobs. (Yes, we actually need $$$$.) Attending a conference offers us a chance to live, eat, and breathe writing—and writing alone—for the duration.

9. *To become inspired.* Conferences are wonderful wellsprings of inspiration. For me, the urge to write powerfully and well is never as strong the rest of the year as it is those first few weeks after a conference.

10. *To love.* Last, but certainly not least, one should attend a conference out of love: Love for one's fellow writers, love of the craft, love of the beauty of words, prose, and ideas with the power to move. I love giving back to others the kind of assistance I received when I was a fledgling writer. These past few years, I've actually been stopped by novices after conference work-shops and told how much my critiques helped them with their projects. What a great feeling of satisfaction that gives me, just knowing I've helped others feel more confident and competent about what they do. We writers work in a lonely, isolated field in which recognition is usually painfully long in coming. Through reaching out and connecting with others like us, we learn to reward each other for work well done.

Writer's Block

Writer's Block

by Jackie Jones

"Write!" I say to the me sitting there, fingers poised over the keyboard. "Will you please get down to business and write?" I think to the me who's just finished playing another game of solitaire.

Nothing. No thoughts worth putting to paper, nothing but silly blather running through my head. Now what?

The muse sits, giggling softly in a dark corner of my mind. It (I'm not at all certain if it's a "she" or a "he") refuses to contribute. It just watches the jumble of words that refuse to become writing, as my fingers skitter over the keyboard.

No lack of story ideas in my head—lots of characters dance around, lots of logical plans for a plot. They all dance there but refuse to be pinned down into a story, especially a story that will be the Great American Novel. They won't settle in for even a short babble; they just dance a bit out of reach.

Take, for instance, that large, unattractive woman sitting on the bar stool, planning the perfect murder. Her thoughts are dark and dingy, but she won't let me close enough to catch them. I see them as red sparks against a black background, swirling around like fireworks, blazing fire-words, but I can't read a one of them. I don't think I like her very much. Could that be part of the problem? Well, I can simply kill her off.

That's one of the wonders of being a writer: the chance to play God, to create or kill as it suits you. I could have the bartender get disgusted with her and feed her cyanide: "You'd like another, eh?" as he reaches below the bar for the ant-and-roach poison. A quick twist of the wrist, a good stir with lemon and rum, and she won't notice a thing until she starts to turn blue. Or he could grab a broken glass and slit her throat, do it with such grace that the patrons of the bar would think it an accident. I wonder if that's been done before?

"Disgusted Bartender Kills Boring Patron!" scream the headlines. Why not?

Sitting there beside her is an elderly man with a halo of white hair framing his sweetly impish face. He peers at the woman through bifocals and licks his lips. Note the fleshy width of his lips, the way they gleam with moisture in the bar's dim light. This little old man is a stalker of women, women he sees as "in need" of his services; he travels the world in search of sexual conquests. He's certain the cure for all female ills is a dose of himself, administered sexually and often. Weighing his chances as he contemplates his own growing interest, he flatters the woman with sidelong glances. Like a bug using its antennae, he tastes the air with his tongue. The woman ignores him.

The bartender is watching this scenario with a very bored expression. He's seen it all before; there is nothing new under his sun. As he polishes a glass, he turns away. This isn't a tale to be told again; it's been told too often. He shrugs this sorry attempt at a story off his mind as a dog shakes off water. In boring him, I've lost my audience. Since that won't do, I must enliven the scene with a bit more interest.

So—the woman jumps up from her chair, throwing her strawberry daiquiri in the face of the elderly gentleman as she shrieks, "Stop looking at me!" He gags, swipes at his dripping face; ice splinters sparkle in his eyebrows. Immediately, a rash forms on his cheeks and forehead—he's violently allergic to strawberries! His tongue protrudes from his mouth as shock sets in, closing his throat. He drops to the floor, claws at his neck; his bulging eyes implore the bartender for help.

The bartender—call him Jake, a burly, laid-back dude from no place in particular and all places in general—strolls around the bar and looks down at the suffering, drink-soaked form. Using the rag from his glass polishing, he wipes the sticky red ice from the man's face.

"Problems should be reported to the management," he intones. "We will not tolerate any messes made on the floor or furniture. Please die elsewhere."

Upon hearing these words of wisdom, the soaked form on the floor rises to the occasion. He brushes off the last of the ice crumbs, takes the arm of the ugly woman, and exits. His death will occur at a later, more appropriate, time and place.

My muse, having dealt me a mixed hand, dozes. In spite of a writer's god-like powers, I decide it's not a good time to give up my day job.

The Reluctant Writer

by Janis Butler Holm

Q: I used to enjoy writing, but now it's become just another job, something I do to increase my income. How can I recover the pleasure I used to feel?

A: One of the most frustrating experiences a writer can have is that of not wanting to write. This stubborn resistance can express itself in any number of ways: a vague feeling of reluctance, a joyless sense of duty, a tendency to procrastinate or to avoid writing tasks, a full-blown writer's block. But whatever the symptoms, the effect of mental mutiny is always the same. When the inner writer refuses to engage, creative processes falter or grind to a painful halt.

Most writers go through cycles of having much to say and then little to say, of racing (or at least chugging) along and then idling afterward. Contemporary writers' books are quick to counsel patience with the uneven rhythms of the writing life. They remind us that much of what we do is an unconscious transaction, not to be forced or controlled, and that learning to accept our irregular progress is a large part of accepting ourselves as creative human beings. At the same time, they tell us to sit down and write something every single day, to keep at it no matter what, to cough up whatever we can until the idling time is over.

Of course, they are absolutely right. Writing when you don't want to write can get you past the not-wanting-to. At least, it can most of the time.

But when it doesn't—when you continue to dread picking up your pen or turning on the computer, when the work is spiritless no matter how long you sit there, when you feel yourself sinking more and more deeply into I-hate-writinghood, when you've felt this way for days and days and days—it may be time to stop trying to write and to start thinking about things.

If you've been writing for extra income and no longer enjoy what you're doing, consider a serious game of Twenty Questions.

— Am I writing about subjects that really interest me?

— Is it time to try a new format? A new genre? A new market?

— Am I failing to challenge myself?

— Is my writing environment conducive to creativity?

— Do I need to change my writing site?

— Do I need to change my writing tools?

— Do I need to change my writing time?

— Am I trying to write when I'm tired or distracted?

— Am I reading enough?

— Am I reading too much?

— Do I need more contact with other writers?

— Am I overloaded? Burned out?

— Are other problems in my life sapping my creativity?

— Am I depressed? Do I need counseling?

— Have I let perfectionism ruin my fun?

- Am I writing too much for others and not enough for myself?

- Have I forgotten how to value my creative efforts?

- Do I need a break from writing?

- Could I make extra money by doing something else for a while?

- Should I try writing for its own sake and forget about the money?

While thinking about the answers, remember that resistance is always a resistance to something. If you can identify that something, whatever it is that continues to block your pleasure, the chances of removing, changing, or working around it are much greater.

But before spending countless hours contemplating your environment and your psyche, take a look at Dorothea Brande's 1934 essay, "The Writer's Recreation." Brande suggests that the writer's fascination with words can lead to overexposure: when writers take time off from writing, they usually find themselves reading, speaking, or listening to words—that is, taking a busman's holiday. To recover the pleasure of writing, she advises, indulge in some *wordless* recreation, preferably alone. Sit on a park bench, take a long walk, listen to music, knit a sweater. In a few hours, Brande explains, the drive to use language will reassert itself; the urge to write will return.

Why not explore this possibility? When writing becomes a chore, go where words can't find you. Avoid all of the agents of discourse (magazines, television, movies, friends, the telephone, e-mail, the Internet) and opt for a wordless solitude. Take a mental furlough while the unconscious does its job. Chances are good that word deprivation will leave you longing for language, that your work will regain its appeal. Like other professions, writing requires regular vacation time, and leaving words behind may be the best way to ensure a happy return.

Brande, Dorothy. *Becoming A Writer*. J. P. Tarcher, 1981 (reprint), ISBN 0-87477-164-1

The Fortitude To Write Without Success

by Rodney Lewis Merrill

As a long-time writer, I've come to see the world as peopled by writers and non-writers. Of course, I hasten to add: "Some of my best friends are non-writers." I go further: I encourage non-writer friends to stay that way. Having too many writer friends is bothersome. At parties, for instance, who would do the listening? And, if I knew only writers, who on earth would I write about? Beyond these few selfish concerns, my advice that non-writers steer clear of writing is purely magnanimous. Writing simply isn't for everyone.

Norman Mailer said: "America is a cruel soil for talent." As a writer, you need a curious sort of courage to sow your destiny in such soil. It takes a certain pluck to commit your fragile soul to paper, then to parade it—unclad—before strangers, most of whom don't give a damn about you, your soul, your talent, or your success. Commercial publishers care about selling publications and selling advertising space within those publications.

Here's how America's cruel soil works, I think, in most publishing companies. If you are "a name"—a commodity—your manuscript gets shuttled directly to a honcho. If you are "a no-name," your fate is decided by a 19-year-old "assistant" trapped "working the slush pile" as part of a university-mandated period of slavery called "journalism internship." Said wretched serf may give your manuscript a 10- or 15-second "pre-read" during his/her "working (i.e. forfeited) lunch" and *if*—despite digestive reflux, anxiety, and smoldering resentment—s/he is willing and able to convince senior editors that your submission is well-written, is consistent with the magazine's style, and (this is probably most important) is less likely than its competitors to piss off underwriters, advertisers, angry white males, still angrier females of all colors, the silent majority, the vocal minorities, secular humanists and fanatic Christians, Muslims, and Jews—congratulations, you'll get published! (Though you must be willing to sell all rights—including all photos and all international, subsidiary, and reprint rights—for $23.50, paid on publication, which averages 3.2 years after acceptance.)

If *not*, your paper proxy crawls back—three-to-six poverty-stricken months later, rumpled and pleated in its anticipatory self-addressed stamped envelope. And it bears the oily heel print of a perfunctory form letter. Your heart exsanguinates. The ensuing anemia, though purely metaphorical, forces you to bed for days, maybe weeks. There you pine for your lost spirit and dashed enthusiasm.

Your corpus callosum short-circuits. You pull the covers over your head and fantasize about a more gratifying life in which your talents, ambitions, and affections lead you to a respectable, financially rewarding vocation like computer programming or garbage collection.

You grow sullen. All attempts at solace fail you—though a whole pound cake topped with a pint of honey-nougat ice cream occasionally comes close. You watch *Stuart Saves His Family* for the sixth time. Only this time when Stuart predicts that he will never save his family but will instead die in a gutter: unknown, unloved, and thirty pounds overweight, you don't laugh. You nod in morose accord.

This malaise usually passes. When it does, you weakly arise from bed and wobble to your desk. There, you press the creases and puckers from your proxy, you dress it up with a deceptively cheerful cover letter, and seal it—and another dollar-and-fifty-cent self-addressed, stamped envelope—within a fresh 10x13. Your wounded heart whimpers "Oh god, please, not again!" but you breath deeply and plunge it—for the tenth, twentieth, fortieth...time—into the postal conduit that leads back into the hostile world of heavy-booted strangers. Again, you wait....

What To Do When Your Story Bogs Down

by Elizabeth Delisi

How many times has this happened to you?

You're working on your latest novel. Everything is going smoothly as page after page, scene after scene click into place. You're feeling pretty smug about the whole thing and are looking forward to typing "The End."

Then it happens. You reach a point about half or two-thirds of the way through the book where suddenly, inexplicably, you're stuck. Blocked. Out of gas. You put your fingers on the keyboard, but nothing comes out. What do you do?

No two books are the same, no two "blocks" are the same, and thus there is no one "magic bullet" solution for this common problem. But there are several things you can try to get the words flowing again—and your story back on track.

One solution is simply to plow ahead, force yourself to sit down in front of the computer and write, regardless of what comes out. Sometimes this works if the problem is simply a lack of confidence. If you experience a "block" in the same place in each novel, then this is probably the cause, and pushing ahead to write an additional chapter or two will shore up your confidence and allow you to continue. However, quite often this approach produces only frustration, not word count.

Taking a break from the work may be what is needed. Choose a book from your "to be read" pile and enjoy it. Go for a walk on the beach, bake some cookies, change the oil on your car—do anything but write. When you feel refreshed in a day or two, return to the book. You may find you have a renewed enthusiasm for the project and are able to jump right in where you left off.

Try discussing the story with a trusted friend or relative. This should be someone who can produce a good suggestion or two, but who is mainly a good listener. Working through the problem out loud can be very useful and can often produce unexpected insights.

Are you working from an outline? If not, try writing one. By the same token, if you are using an outline but your story has diverged from it, try rewriting the outline from your "blocked" point forward. An outline can be of great comfort because it means you always have somewhere to go with the plot and are never "painted into a corner." But remember: you aren't bound by the outline—it exists simply to help you proceed when you're not sure where to go, to give you confidence in yourself and in your story.

Try writing a scene that occurs later in the book, preferably one that has some excitement and movement to it. Sometimes this nonchronological leap can revive your enthusiasm in the project and allow you to return to the "blocked" scene with renewed vigor.

Sometimes a writer loses interest partwaythrough a book because the idea for another book has come to him. This newer, fresher idea insists on being given attention, but he feels guilty about abandoning the current project—a sure recipe for writer's block! If a fresh idea is the cause of your "block," stop working on your current project long enough to jot down a few notes about the new story—brief character sketches, main plot points, the ending if you know it—so that the idea won't be lost. Once you've done that, return to the original project and take up the work again.

Unfortunately, your writing may have bogged down because there is an underlying problem with the book. It may be that you're trying to force your hero to do something out of character, the plot has become unbeliev-able or unwieldy, or the sequence of events is out of order. Here are a few suggestions that may help you uncover the problem.

If you are working from an outline, try changing the sequence of events that come next. Jot down the next few scenes on index cards, one scene to a card. Lay them out on your dining room table or living room floor, and then rearrange them. Does a different sequence make more sense? If so, then you've found your problem and can return to your writing.

Try skipping the next scene and writing ahead from there. If the writing goes smoothly, then perhaps the scene you were trying to write isn't really necessary. You may simply need to insert a sentence or two of transition, or work the necessary information into the next few scenes in bits and pieces.

The middle of the book can seem like the most boring part of the story. The characters and their conflicts have been introduced, but it's not yet time for the climax. Mickey Friedman, author of the mysteries *A Temporary Ghost, Magic Mirror,* and *Venetian Mask,* has said that, whenever her story bogs down in the middle, she has her heroine kidnapped. This doesn't mean you must literally have your character kidnapped, but it does mean you should liven things up. Add an action scene or two. Put your hero in danger. Throw another monkey wrench into the works. Do whatever is necessary to keep things lively.

If you've tried all of the above suggestions and are still blocked, it may be that you're just not ready to write this particular story. Lawrence Block, in *Writing Mysteries: A Handbook by the Mystery Writers of America,* tells of finding two thirty-page sections of manuscripts he'd written and abandoned years ago.

> "Well, I read both of those chunks of manuscript, and I was amazed. I don't have a clue what I thought was wrong with them at the time I stopped work on them...all either manuscript lacked to be perfectly publishable was another 270 pages in the same vein. Looking back, it strikes me as highly probable that I would have been incapable of producing those 270 pages back then."

If you feel this is the case, you may just have to put the book aside in your "better-to-have-written-and-blocked-than-never-to-have-written-at-all" file and chalk it up to experience. After all, no one ever has said that being a writer is easy.

Lawrence Block in *Writing Mysteries: A Handbook by the Mystery Writers of America,* edited by Sue Grafton; Writer's Digest Books, Cincinnati, Ohio, 1992

Inspiration

*Eventually I realized
that the paintings
worked because I let the
paints become what
they wanted to be.*

Visual And Verbal Communication

by Laura Bagby

My mother is an artist. I am a writer. I thought I was *only* a writer until, by chance, I took up painting with watercolors six years ago. In fact, I had always stated unequivocally that I was *not* an artist and that I couldn't draw a stick figure, much less the proverbial straight line.

During a time when I was staying home to write full time (read that: unemployed), my best friend's young daughter stayed with me for a week. She was much younger than my own children and I worked hard to come up with things to keep her busy. We colored computer-generated designs for several days.

After she went home, I continued to color designs as a way of avoiding the writing I knew I should do while I had the time. I started to draw my own designs and to experiment with color combinations. In a desperate attempt to overcome writer's block and depression, I got out the watercolors and brushes my mother had given me the year before. These gifts had made me laugh when I received them since I had no intention of trying to use them. But during this time of exploration, I was desperate to overcome the mental obstacles to my writing; this desperation led me to do the one thing I had always said I could not do: create visual art.

The beautiful fuchsias and turquoises dripped off my brush onto wet paper and dissolved my depression. I became so engrossed in producing new colors and ways to put color on paper that I did not take time to write. I sat at my folding table late into each night, colors swirling in front of me like dreams on closed eyelids. The paints arranged themselves on the paper in ways I had never before imagined.

Eventually I realized that the paintings worked because I let the paints become what they wanted to be. In the process, I supplied the medium for them to develop into a visual expression. That license was what had been missing from my writing; I had been trying too hard, forcing the words to be exactly what I wanted them to be, what I expected them to be. My expectations were the major problem; I expected to write well in the first draft even though I was an expert in teaching process writing.

On the other hand, I certainly had no expectations when it came to visual expression. If anything, my expectation was that it would be a pleasant way to pass the time but nothing valuable would come from this activity. Instead, I produced art that shocked me with its visual eloquence. Since I was a highly verbal person, I was astonished that I could communicate without words.

Although I was communicating in a completely non-verbal manner, I was communicating almost the same emotions and ideas in paint that I did in my poetry. The painting came more easily, though, because I was more willing to let the paints arrange themselves than I was the words in a poem. When I applied the same method to my writing that I had discovered in my painting, the words became as colorful as my paint palette. The ideas were as fluid as the water that flowed across my hot-pressed watercolor paper.

That winter I did some remarkable writing that I attribute directly to my experimentation with watercolor. Because watercolor cannot be tightly controlled, it is the perfect medium for learning how to release the left side of one's brain in order to allow the right side to create exciting new modes of articulation. When I convey an emotion or an idea in a nonverbal mode, that process helps me to verbalize in truly original ways.

I now understand that I am a creative person and that all my visual and verbal communications are interrelated. When I get painter's block, I write for a while, and when I get writer's block, I paint until I can again approach my writing with a fresh perspective. I display my art in local shows, and people have begun to recognize me as a visual artist. I am still a writer—but a more colorful, creative writer than I used to be.

> *Many great stories have at least some basis*
> *in fact, but they work primarily because*
> *the author has learned the difference*
> *between truth and reality.*

Five Mistakes
Beginning Writers Make
And How To Avoid Them

by Gwenneth Barnes

1. *Not reading*

Reading widely, often, and well is the key to understanding and writing successfully for your audience.

Make it a point to read good books by good writers, both inside and outside your chosen genre. Don't read just for entertainment or information—read thoughtfully, and be conscious of the way the best writers use words: not just for their meaning, but for their flavor and rhythm as well.

Read bad books, too—even trashy drugstore novels can teach you much about your craft. The structures of plot, narrative, and dialogue are very close to the surface in these books, so those elements are easy to see. Note the clichés, the formulas, and the predictability of these stories, and, at the same time, note that even with these shortcomings, these books "work" at the right level to attract a loyal readership.

2. *Not writing*

Wanting to be a writer is like wanting to be rich, or thin, or beautiful. Is your goal realistic? Are you taking steps now to make your dreams happen, or are you relying on luck to get you where you want to go? Even with hard work and genuine talent, not everyone who deserves fame, beauty or wealth gets it.

Your goal should be to write something, anything, every day, faithfully and without fail. If you're not naturally prolific, like Joyce Carol Oates or Stephen King, use external motivators: make a commitment to write articles for your local community paper, for instance, or get involved in a writing workshop that requires you to bring new work to every meeting.

If you're having trouble getting started, try some of the exercises in *Steering The Craft*, Ursula LeGuin's excellent guide for young writers. She uses (and demands) practical examples, not just abstract theory, to demonstrate her points.

3. Only writing "what you know"

Beginning writers are often advised, even by people who ought to know better, to "write what you know." Better advice would be "write what's true, whether or not it really happened." Many great stories have at least some basis in fact, but they work primarily because the author has learned the difference between truth and reality.

Anecdotes typically don't make good fiction, even if they "really happened that way." Real events are often unbelievable in the fictional sense, which is why a new author will sometimes hear the criticism that a story is "too true to be good." Try rearranging a character here, a detail there, and see if that adds the necessary fictional truth to a real story.

In fiction, truth and reality have meanings different from what they have in the real world. A writer has told the truth when the reader believes that a fictional scene must have, or could have, happened, whether or not the scene has any basis in objective fact.

4. Not inviting your audience into your stories

There is nothing wrong with writing purely for yourself: to get something off your chest, or to express feelings privately that you cannot comfortably share with another soul. That is not creative writing, however; it is therapy, and many beginning writers demonstrate a lack of awareness of that distinction. They don't include their audience in their stories.

If your goal as a writer is recognition and publication, you are writing for an audience, and that audience has certain basic rights and expectations. You can, in fact, think of your readers as characters in their own right. They must be properly developed if your story is going to work. Just like your characters, your readers should not be manipulated in one direction or another, forced to act or feel anything that is not genuine and proper for them.

Your goal, through writing, is to tell the world what it's like to be "you," the fictional narrator. Does your audience want something comforting and familiar, or do they want to experience something entirely different from their own lives? Create roles in your stories for the kinds of readers you wish to reach.

5. Not hearing, seeing, and feeling the world around you

You must be able to describe objectively how you feel about something before your characters can express any of their feelings convincingly. This means you must not only be intimately familiar with your own repertoire of emotions, you must also be able to stand apart from yourself and honestly observe and describe the contents of your psyche.

Beginning writers often suffer from a kind of abstraction that indicates a basic unawareness of the world around them or within them. At their worst, the feelings they express are about as personal and relevant as the greeting card rack at the drugstore. More commonly, their stories sound vague and secondhand.

John Gardner, in his books *The Art of Fiction* and *On Becoming a Novelist*, considers this secondhand emotion a kind of frigidity, a basic and incurable defect in a writer's character. (I think Gardner goes to this extreme partly to shock his students into proving they are not among the guilty.) Whatever its source, this kind of abstraction must be omitted from your prose. Use all your senses to notice and describe details within a scene. Show how it feels to be each of your characters, to experience their pleasures and anxieties. Include details that make your settings unique, memorable, and authentic.

LeGuin, Ursula. *Steering the Craft*. Eighth Mountain Press, 1998, ISBN: 0933377460

Gardner, John. *The Art Of Fiction*. Vintage Books, 1991 (reissue), ISBN: 0679734031

Gardner, John. *On Becoming A Novelist*. W.W. Norton & Company, 1999 (paper), ISBN: 0393320030

Most writers find the language they need
more easily once basic ideas have been
articulated.

Unintentional Plagiarism

by Janis Butler Holm

Q: Recent news stories about romance writer Janet Dailey's plagiarizing from Nora Roberts have left me uneasy. I would never choose to copy anyone else's work, but how do I make sure that I don't borrow unconsciously? How can I prevent unintentional plagiarism?

A: You've raised an interesting question. Though often entwined with legal questions of copyright infringement, plagiarism is primarily an ethical issue. It has to do with how we treat one another and whether we can respect the achievements of people not ourselves. As everyone knows, the ethically sound writer does not set out to poach another's work. But the creative process is mysterious and often unwitting, sometimes with problematic consequences.

In literary matters, the definition of plagiarism is fairly clear: claiming another writer's language and/or line of thinking as one's own. From the Latin term *plagiarius*, meaning plunderer or kidnapper, "plagiarism" denotes artistic theft: stealing the results of inventive labor. In most writerly circles, such theft is unforgivable. It's the tackiest of sins.

Some forms of plagiarism are obvious, as in the extensive appropriation of passages, concepts, and/or plots. In these cases, the offending writer is usually perceived as having plagiarized on purpose, since prolonged states of unconscious cribbing are hardly the norm. However, Janet Dailey's defense, her claim that her acts of copying reflect a psychological disorder, reminds us that some kinds of stealing may be beyond the control of the stealer. As Alexander Lindey observed in 1952, the compulsive plagiarist "is a kleptomaniac" and is just as medically afflicted as the compulsive liar or compulsive arsonist.

Most intentional plagiarism is subtle, crafty. Most plagiarists take steps to conceal their theft, to make it more difficult to detect or to prove. They may lift the design but not the content, reorganize themes into new configurations, compose a pastiche from multiple sources, or embellish a paraphrase with gems of their own. The results may be dazzling—plagiarism can be highly original, even as it depends on reproduction. The persistent plagiarist is often a con artist, a sneak thief, someone who takes pride in the heist.

Another form of plagiarism is generated by indifference or carelessness, as in "I could not care less." In this case, the writer does not bother to keep track of sources, or neglects to credit other authors, or believes that he or she, having superior talent, is naturally entitled to exploit the work of lesser talent. Plagiarists of this kind are narcissistic, oblivious to others as real persons with creative claims, and they tend to view other people's writing as fodder, rather than as creative work in its own right. Lacking ego boundaries, the narcissist finds it hard to appreciate others' rights of ownership.

But plagiarism isn't always, or even usually, an act of pathology or severe ethical dysfunction. More often it's the doing of the average person, the writer who knows better, who understands creative limits, but who chooses to plagiarize in a moment of weakness or stress. Greed, ambition, envy, perfectionism, anxiety—there are any number of ordinary human pressures that may tempt a writer to cheat. When Janet Dailey points to her husband's cancer and the deaths of two brothers as among the stresses that led her to plagiarize two of Nora Roberts's books in the early '90s, she is suggesting that multiple pressures led to multiple moments of temptation, to which she unfortunately succumbed. (Roberts, pointing to the plagiarism of a third book in the late '90s, sees Dailey's copying not as a short string of transgressive moments but as a sustained modus operandi.)

Whether the effect of pathology, momentary weakness, or a calculated M.O., plagiarism violates the rights of the author and establishes the plagiarist as a traitor to the profession. Its impact can be devastating. Consequently, savvy writers take pains to avoid not only literary theft per se but whatever might seem to be derivative of another author's work. They are also on guard against unintentional plagiarism, those accidents of research or memory that make someone else's invention feel like one's own.

How can we keep from plagiarizing unintentionally? To begin with, we can recognize the nature of our debt to writers who have preceded us. Much of a writer's language and knowledge comes from reading; none of us creates without building on what has come before. But when we produce original work, that work reflects a process of invention and transformation. It offers newness and difference, not a simple shuffling of others' words and concepts. We are necessarily indebted to the writers who have taught us, but we ought not borrow more than is fair. And fairness requires monitoring, since much of the work of writing happens without our being aware of the origins of our words and ideas.

If you wish to avoid unintentional plagiarism, consider the following.

— Trust your own voice.

Many writers, hitting a snag in the writing process, reach for the work of other writers. While reading an admired author can be inspiring, doing so when desperate for language can lead to trouble. If you are suffering through a period when words won't come, try getting away from language altogether, at least for a time. (Go for a stroll, or clean out a closet.) If the problem is that you don't think your words sufficiently colorful or precise, write out what you have to say in your own voice despite your misgivings. Most writers find the language they need more easily once basic ideas have been articulated.

— When researching a topic, take careful notes.

When writing requires research, be consistent and systematic in your note-taking. Put quotation marks around direct quotations (and record page numbers). Otherwise, as time passes, it will become increasingly difficult to remember which words are yours and which are not, or exactly where you found the material you wish to quote. When paraphrasing material in your notes, avoid following the language of your source too closely. And be sure to develop a system for distinguishing between source material and those brainstorms that can occur while reading someone else's prose; some writers mark their personal responses with "me" or their first initial, followed by a colon. Keep a record of which sources you use and when.

Once you've finished a writing project, review your notes to be sure you haven't unconsciously lifted a choice phrase or idea.

— Allow plenty of time for work before deadlines.

Although procrastination can induce a productive adrenaline rush, original writing may take time. Last-minute work isn't always good work, and the writer who is down to the wire may be frantic and so less mindful of creative boundaries. Avoid panic and consequent recklessness by beginning projects early. Give yourself time to form your own approach, your own concepts, your own language.

— Distinguish between information that is common knowledge (or a matter of observation or experience) and information that requires documentation.

Facts, beliefs, etc. that are widely known or available in basic reference sources need not be documented. For example, information about the Latin roots of the word "plagiarism," provided near the beginning of this essay, is readily available in both English and Latin dictionaries; no citation is necessary. Likewise, the subsequent discussion of types of plagiarists, because it is based on the author's observations, requires no documentation. The categories offered represent the writer's conceptual scheme, not material from outside sources.

On the other hand, the idea that the compulsive plagiarist suffers from a kind of kleptomania is attributed to Alexander Lindey because the observation is his, not the author's. Though Lindey's point could be said to be a matter of common sense, it is not a matter of common knowledge—except, perhaps, among some defense attorneys and medical specialists, who are not the primary audience for this essay.

If you use information that is not common knowledge but that appears in several sources, cite the earliest source in which you find it.

— Do unto others....

Above all, exercise professional courtesy. Be generous in acknowledging your debts, and don't take more than you would have others take from your own work. When the pressure is on, remember that you are part of a larger creative community, one in which respect for others' efforts is both highly valued and necessary. Remember, too, that there is tremendous pleasure in having created work that is scrupulously your own.

Lindey, Alexander. *Plagiarism And Originality.* Harper, 1952

*In effect, writers who try haiku may discover more
than the pleasures of a new artistic form.*

Why Try Haiku?

by Janis Butler Holm

Q : I'm a fiction writer who would like to try poetry. A friend of mine
has suggested that I begin with haiku, but I don't know much
about this genre. Can you tell me something about it?

A: One of the world's briefest poetic forms, haiku (pronounced "hi coo")
is native to Japan, where it reached the peak of its development during the
seventeenth century. Originally the opening verse of a longer poetic sequence, the haiku became widely recognized as an independent literary unit
after the work of Matsuo Basho (1644-1694), best known to Westerners as
the Shakespeare of haiku. Basho, from an old samurai family, studied poetry as a youth; later he established a literary school in Edo (now Tokyo),
became a devoted follower of Zen Buddhism, and wrote poetry and prose
in a variety of forms. His disciples and subsequent admirers continued the
haiku tradition after his death.

The traditional Japanese haiku is minimalist, direct, and concrete. In
plain but evocative language, it focuses on the oneness of nature and hu-
mankind, primarily through a tangible natural image (or two) meant to
convey a moment of insight and clarity. That is, as in the Zen moment of
enlightenment, the nature of a natural phenomenon is contemplated in its
fullness.

On a withered branch
a crow has settled—
autumn nightfall.
(Basho, translated by Harold G. Henderson)

The haiku does not announce an intended meaning. It does not analyze or provide commentary. Instead, it suggests by association, inviting the reader to complete its meaning. (Is autumn nightfall like a crow? Are we, like the crow, small against the night? Do "withered," "crow," "autumn," and "nightfall" characterize old age? Do not we, like nature, vary in our seasons?) Haiku are usually composed without metaphors or similes; relationships are drawn instead by juxtaposition, by placing images next to one another.

Typically, the haiku stanza averages 17 Japanese phonetic characters, broken into a rhythm of 5, 7, and 5, without rhymed endings. Because Japanese phonetics and English phonetics are significantly different (generally, Japanese is spoken more quickly than is English), it is sometimes difficult to capture the brevity and sharpness of Japanese haiku in 17 English syllables. Nonetheless, a number of poets, whether translating or writing original poems, aim for a 5-7-5 syllable structure.

A bitter morning:
sparrows sitting together
without any necks.
(James W. Hackett)

Others, pointing to variations from the 5-7-5 pattern within the Japanese haiku tradition, focus on rendering images as succinctly as possible, as in the translation of Basho above and in the poem below.

walking the snow crust
not sinking
sinking
(Anita Virgil)

In each poem quoted here, the author has taken care to include a seasonal reference, another characteristic of traditional haiku. Seventeenth-century poetry handbooks included lists of words linked to specific seasons. "Cherry blossoms," "evening shower," "fallen leaves," "withering wind," and similar words and phrases functioned as a kind of poetic shorthand, a way of evoking a cluster of seasonal associations in very little space.

Composing haiku is a wise practice for both poets and prose writers, as the demands of its structure force us to condense our language, sharpen our images, and focus our sensory perception. And the product of that work, the poem itself, has a meditative value that is rare in Western writing. It records and elicits a kind of contemplation that is absent from most of our literary experience. In effect, writers who try haiku may discover more than the pleasures of a new artistic form. Some discover nothing less than a new relation to the surrounding world.

FURTHER READING

The three poems quoted above appear, respectively, in the following books, all of which provide useful introductions to haiku:

Henderson, Harold G. *An Introduction To Haiku*. Doubleday, 1958, p. 18

Giroux, Joan. *The Haiku Form*. Tuttle, 1974, ISBN 0804811105, p. 120

Higginson, William J. and Penny Harter. *The Haiku Handbook*. McGraw-Hill, 1985, ISBN 0070287864, p. 170.

Self-Discipline And Self-Motivation

by Rodney Lewis Merrill

Like others, I've played the flighty artist-writer. I've waited for the in-spirational mule to kick me in the ass and get me started. Waiting for the muse-mule is a lark. It's as fun as wearing nautical garb on a skiff or a beret to art class.

It's also horseshit. Writing is not magic. It's not mystical. Writing is hard work.

Inventor-genius Thomas Edison said, "Creative genius is 1% inspira-tion and 99% perspiration." Nobel Prize-winning writer Richard Rhodes credits much of his success to an early mentor—Conrad Knickerbocker—who offered this crusty advice on writing inspiration: "Rhodes, you apply ass to chair."

Alacazam! It works for me.

"Applying ass to chair" lets "your muse" know you're ready to work. Any "magic" comes from stipulating a writing habit and sticking to it. This is easier for some and near to impossible for others, but it—not magic—is the key to writing. If you are to write—as opposed to fantasizing about it—you must find a time and place for writing. Then, short of a stock market crash or armed revolt, you must write.

Habit follows repetition. For this reason, writing at the same time and place each day is best. I often schedule my writing around the 50-minute clothes dryer cycle. Once I twist that "start" knob, the dryer manages quite well without me. And after a 50 minute cycle, I'm ready for a break. I "remove clothes promptly for best results" as instructed by the silver sticker on the dryer door, then strew them across the bed so they can cool down. (Who am I kidding? I hate folding laundry and I'm simply procrastinating.) Then I go back to writing.

Midday, I go to the kitchen and scratch together a huge pot of something—spaghetti sauce, pea soup, scalloped potatoes—anything that can simmer until dinner time. If I believed in a writer's muse (other than habit), I'd posit mine in the kitchen cutting boards. A few moments of uninhibited carnage—slashing my way through defenseless members of the plant kingdom with freshly sharpened cold-forged steel—and my writing takes off like a prairie fire in an updraft!

You need a month to establish a new habit. If the new practice differs dramatically from your normal life, you may need a little longer. The trick is not to quit. Even if you miss now and then, get discouraged, and take to bed with pound cake and ice cream, pull yourself together as soon as you can and get back to work.

A Zen saying: Fall down seven times, stand up eight.

Keep at it. Even if falling down and standing up becomes a habit with you, it beats falling down and staying down.

If you have trouble getting started, don't wait around for omens and muses (commonly known as "pissing into the wind"). Do something. Apply the "99% perspiration" part of Edison's formula. Write about why you want to write, what you hope to accomplish by writing, or how it feels when you sit down to write and find the word-well is bleached bones dry. Write about how your ass gets unbearably sore the minute you run out of words—discomfiting you as to their source.

It makes no difference what you write. The important thing is that you write. And write. And write. Every appointed day.

Generate boxes and boxes of really stinky stuff. Mound them into great putrescent heaps. In writing, compost and bilge water contain the tiny seeds from which you can root and nurture a lush fruiting tree.

In the beginning, the habit is more important than attainment. What you accomplish with your commitment of time and place is secondary to honoring the promise. Apply ass to chair. Write. These are achievements enough.

Humor

Plug Nickels From Sea To Shining Sea (or) Don't Let This Happen to You.

by Rodney Lewis Merrill

*I*f I had a nickel for each and every time I tossed in a cliché on the spur of the moment, when, beyond a shadow of a doubt, I should have held it in abeyance, I'd have a shot at the gold for the hands-down king of this fool's paradise we call writing.

By the same token, I can say in deadly earnest that there's a method in my madness: it stands to reason that, all things considered, a well-turned cliché—said with tongue in cheek—is, in the final analysis, far and away a force to be reckoned with. A bone-tired cliché may be nothing to write home about, but it doesn't deserve the unsavory reputation it holds in some circles nowadays.

I have a healthy respect for the cliché. I find that, in the long run, using the well-chosen cliché is half the battle in turning the tide of opinion among the general reading public. Still and all, you don't want to go overboard and have a cliché free-for-all. Clichés aren't meant to be tossed about, willy-nilly, in any and all circumstances. When the cliché becomes a crutch, it can become more of a stumbling block than a help.

I have grave concerns, though, about letting the powers that be lay down the law about never using a cliché. I'm bound and determined not to let this miscarriage of justice happen. You can't just, willy-nilly, make hard-and-fast rules like that. But I say the burden of proof is on those who want to eighty-six them. Clichés are a fact of life for the foreseeable future, and they serve their purpose. Banning them should be a last resort, when things are completely out of hand and you've reached a point of no return.

All around, I'd say those who try to outlaw the cliché are their own worst enemies. Close scrutiny will show that, should the untimely death of the cliché come to light, the great unwashed would revolt so quickly that it would make your head swim. There would be such a hue and cry over hill and dale, from every mountaintop, from sea to shining sea, that the self-styled gurus would have a fast-and-furious change of heart. They would have no choice but to mend their ways.

The common man has a heart of gold. He will tolerate death and taxes by virtue of necessity. He will tolerate a ban on smoking in public places because it's a blessing in disguise. But take away his cliché without rhyme or reason, and he'll come unglued. He'll tell you in no uncertain terms that the cliché is the heart and soul of our do-or-die culture.

Whether the cliché is 100 percent proper is neither here nor there. I wouldn't give a plugged nickel for proper. The cliché is tried and true. That's the thing. It is hard and fast. And it is short and sweet. The cliché says what needs to be said in less than no time.

Last but not least, let me take this parting shot. A glass can be seen as half empty or half full. I, for one, prefer to see it as half full. In other words, it may be the cliché's eleventh hour, but it's only the eleventh hour. It's not over 'til the fat lady sings.

Let's get down to brass tacks, shall we? Tomorrow is another day. Another full day. And it's the first day of the rest of our lives. I feel the winds of change beneath my wings and have great expectations that, tomorrow, the cliché will rise up like a Phoenix from its own ashes and get a new lease on life.

I see no reason for fear and trembling. We can save the cliché if only we put our minds to it.

This is our moment of truth. This is the acid test. Can we avail ourselves of this golden opportunity to find that silver lining behind the cloud of naysayers and gloomy Guses? That is the burning question.

I know we can. Surely, here, in the richest and most powerful country on earth, if we can put a man on the moon, we can come together in a bipartisan effort. We can put aside our differences. We can pull ourselves up by our bootstraps, from the depths of despair to the heights of achievement. Surely, we can put on our thinking caps and agree to disagree.

Deep-down inside, we are one and the same. We can do all this and more if only we can raise ourselves above our petty differences.

Friends, my heart is as light as a feather because I know we can. And I have high hopes that we will. Tomorrow is going to be a brighter day.

Thank you. God bless you. And God bless America.

Humor:
The System

by Jeremiah Gilbert

Attention fiction writers. We all know how difficult it is to find the time to write, between employment, family and other countless responsibilities, but do you realize how much time goes into just preparing to write? Plots, characters' names and backgrounds, tone, voice, symbolism—every element of writing requires abundant amounts of precious time before even one word is put on the page. We at Surrogate Writing Systems have developed a comprehensive program to eliminate these time consuming obstacles, leaving you more time to pursue what's most important to you.

That's right, with The System (patent pending), you can free yourself of unneeded writerly worries. First, The System allows you to choose from one of fifty master plots, so you'll never have to worry about what your characters will do next. Choose from grand epic plots of lust, greed and adventure, or perhaps a simple maiden-in-distress story.

Each plot has a standard number of established characters, but you can vary that if you like (this is not recommended). Once you've chosen the number, The System will automatically name each character appropriately, establishing a history not only for each character, but between characters. No more filling out index cards or charting relations on graphs.

Concerned your characters will be too similar? With our exclusive Diversify feature, you can fill your tales with Christians and pagans, Liberals and Conservatives, environmentalists and lumberjacks. Just let The System know how diverse you want your characters to be and it will use the latest

Census data to statistically ensure a culturally, economically, and spiritually diverse fictional populace.

Now that the What and Who have been established, The System can move you into the ideal opening scene. Decide if you'd prefer first, second or third person and the tense, and you're on your way. Or if you'd rather, The System will randomly select a style and tense for you (recommended). Then tell The System how many subplots you'd like (every master plot has at least one hundred subplots to choose from, all interrelated for your convenience) and sit back as scene after scene writes itself.

Stuck for a title? No problem. The System has been established to generate many titles, from simple, easy to remember monosyllabic titles to cryptic Shakespearean references. Feel in a literary mood? Then choose a hefty title. The System has no limits to title length or complexity, though a recommended length and syllable count for your chosen story will be suggested.

Concerned about voice? All writers struggle to establish their own unique voice, but with The System, there's no need for this. Once your basic story is generated, go into our Styles room and chose from countless writing styles. Selections include Biblical (King James Version), Joycean (complete with made-up words and obscure geographical references), Faulknerian (with sentences so long you'll forget where they began), and Hemingway-esque (not an adjective or adverb in sight). Or choose from one of our many "bestseller" styles, where even the flimsiest of stories can be taken to novel length with vast amounts of fluff.

Once your story is complete, send it to our special Markets Finder, listing every paying market for the writing produced by The System. If you don't have such a list, the Market Finder will automatically generate a list of markets for you and even produce a convenient cover letter. Of course, the copyright for any piece generated using The System is retained by Surrogate Writing Systems and all payments are made to us, with a small percent sent to you for taking the effort to mail the story, but these are minor technicalities when one is on the road to becoming a published author.

Yes, with The System, you can finally find that time to write by letting us do the writing. And if you act now we'll include our special BioMaker, so when success comes knocking, you'll have a stellar biography to include with your writing. Choose from a humble, self-taught background, or impress your old flames with an Ivy League history.

With The System and BioMaker, no story is impossible.

If you do all these things during your next conference appointment, I guarantee you'll make quite an impression.

Editor/Agent Appointment Etiquette

by Bridget Anderson

*I*f you're headed to a writer's conference this summer, boy, have I got some tips for you. After sitting through many of these over the years, I've learned a thing or two. Here's how I wisely use my fifteen minutes to pitch my novel. If you follow these tips, you're sure to make a lasting impression on every editor or agent you meet.

1. Wear comfortable attire for your appointment. Try your favorite jeans and a tee-shirt or sweatshirt. And, of course, a pair of sneakers. If you're not comfortable in jeans, then by all means wear your favorite sundress. After all, the interviewer will be comfortable—shouldn't you be?

2. If you really want to be remembered, arrive about ten minutes late. You want to make a grand entrance. Trust me, your audience will never forget you.

3. Take this time to find out as much as you can about the person interviewing you. Ask a few personal questions-they help to break the ice. Ask for guidelines for the genre you want to write in.

4. Bring your completed manuscript, ready to hand out. You never know—editors and agents may need some reading for the plane ride home.

5. Be ready to pitch your story as if you were telling it to a friend. Don't leave any stones unturned. Ignore the time; your story is too good to be squeezed into fifteen minutes.

6. If you haven't finished the manuscript, by all means don't let the interviewer know. Say that it's complete, and then go home and write like crazy.

7. Be sure to have a stack of business cards ready to hand out to everyone you meet. Before your appointment is over, give the editor or agent your card and ask for hers. If you don't have one, write your information down on the closest napkin you can find. Don't worry about whether she will keep it; she'll find a good place for it.

8. Make sure you have a pad and pencil for writing down everything said during the session. There's no way you'll remember it all later.

9. When the editor or agent stands, signaling it's time for you to leave, politely stand up and give her a big hug. The show of affection will be greatly appreciated.

If you do all these things during your next conference appointment, I guarantee you'll make quite an impression. In fact, you'll be the primary topic of conversation when your interviewers return to work. After all, how many opportunities do they have to hear about work like yours?

Genre Writing

Historical

Thoughts On Researching Historical Novels

by Peggy Ullman Bell

Many fine men and women have devoted their lives and careers to researching and publishing historical reference material. We owe them our respect, and, as writers of historical fiction, we owe it to ourselves, and our readers to make our stories as historically accurate as possible. We should never carelessly scramble history to suit our stories.

Does this mean that we cannot adjust the facts to suit our plot? Well, yes—and no. Please note that I said, "carelessly." Most historical novelists have toyed with history for the sake of plot movement. However, the best do not do it carelessly. The trick is to know exactly what you are moving and to be painstakingly certain that you portray events within the time period accurately.

One way to avoid problems with historical events and personages is to write "between" the facts. Say, for instance, that information about the beginning and the outcome of an event is readily available, but your extensive research turns up nothing about the middle. Does that mean you can do whatever you want with the middle? Pretty much. Just don't kill off anyone known to have been around for the end.

Sometimes all you want is the flavor of a historical era. That is sometimes harder to deal with than events. For example, how do people care for their clothes? How do they cook their food? How do they handle sanitation, disease, birth control, and a thousand other details of everyday life?

The important thing is that you do not have your characters using something they could not have had at the time your story supposedly takes place.

The first fan letter I ever wrote was to an author, berating him for an anachronism in his novel. Every time I write, I remember that and try to write for any other ten-year-old scholar who might pick up one of my books one day. I have found that the best way for me to avoid those chastising fan letters is by intensively studying a previous era.

For one of my novels, I needed to know whether flat irons existed in the nineteenth century. My research of the eighteenth century proved their existence in that era. Therefore, it was a pretty good bet that my female lead would have used a flat iron in the nineteenth. Of course, setting a novel in nineteenth century America makes for easy research. So much information is available that knowing when to stop researching and to start writing becomes difficult.

Now is a good time to start writing the novel, whenever now is. "Never" is the perfect time to stop researching. I find myself doing additional spot research through multiple rewrites, as almost everything I change must be checked for accuracy.

What if your story wants to happen in an unresearchable era? Then it becomes essential to research previous times. It behoves us, as writers of good fiction, to spend the time and effort necessary to check and recheck all material we use from the past—or to leave history strictly alone and write our fiction without the help of research and researchers. We cannot shrug and say, "The historical setting is such a small part of the novel that it doesn't matter." History matters a lot to your readers, or they wouldn't be reading historical novels.

If you have good reason to believe that the situation in which you want to put a character could not have happened in the time and place you wish it to have happened, it is you and your character who must adjust—history cannot.

Writing The Memoir

by Victoria Benson

The very nature of the memoir makes it unique. Each person's life is like no other's, and our impressions of our life experiences differs from anyone else's memories of the same events. The unique emotional slant that each individual places on her own significant happenings is what distinguishes a memoir from an autobiography.

In her article, "From Memory to Memoir," in the February, 1999 issue of *Writers Digest Magazine,* Mimi Schwartz writes that the memoir "transforms fragments of memory into what a life means." It is not important that the author remember details, but rather that she makes a connection between those details and how they have affected her future choices, tastes and responses.

In the same article, Frank McCourt, author of *Angela's Ashes*, says, "An autobiography is an attempt at factual reconstruction of events. A memoir is an impression of events, the gist of conversation, if not the precise language."

Not purely history, yet not fiction, the memoir resembles a painting from the Impressionist era of the late nineteenth century. Before that time, artists painted reproductions of life around them using controlled lighting, always indoors. This style of art is Realism and parallels the autobiography in writing.

A small group of French artists bravely changed the way we look at art by giving the viewer a sense, or feel, of how something looked to the artist, rather than a realistic copy. Because of each artist's unique style, we have an idea how they felt about each scene they painted. A cluster of colored dots, a streak, a slash or a splash of color—these represent the out-of-doors world they courageously chose to capture on canvas.

The memoir accomplishes the same purpose. Just as the French Impressionists implemented primary colors and short brush strokes to simulate the play of light on their subjects, the author of the memoir focuses her strokes on the details that colored her memories.

Frank McCourt advises us not to prepare an outline to flesh out a memoir as we would a novel. Memoirs do not work that way. We will have a general idea of our story and the important events, but they won't speak to us of their significance until we begin to write. That is when the human mind performs its wonders, when conversations, smells, and flashes of long-forgotten memories leap into our consciousness. Then the theme and the full scope of our work will start to appear. Often, these revelations will occur after we've written a good portion of our story, and we will need to go back and rearrange our manuscript again and again. But the end result will reward us with its richness and depth.

This procedure is vastly different from revising fiction, or even standard nonfiction, in which the plot or purpose is defined from the start. In a memoir, the author usually doesn't know what theme will speak the loudest as it weaves around others throughout the story.

"Plot is not something imposed on a story, but something organic, rising from the material itself," says Jane Taylor McDonnell in *Living To Tell The Tale: A Guide To Writing Memoir*. She continues, "The story is a given, something found in life itself; the plot is the shape the story must eventually take, and it may not be obvious at first."

The stories, settings and characters are already provided for us. What makes these elements a memoir rather than an autobiography is not what happened but why it is significant. We must ask ourselves if our reaction to these situations made sense under the circumstances. If the answer is "no," then we have a compelling reason to figure it out and write about it. Most people wonder at their own reactions to certain stimuli in their lives. For instance, why did I develop a sudden fear of heights at sixteen? Why is it so important that you cook ham rather than turkey at Thanksgiving?

While researching and writing my husband's memoir, *To No Man's Glory*, I discovered the roots of his current idiosyncrasies. When he first arises in the morning, before I can cook breakfast, he fixes himself two pieces of plain toast. He doesn't do this out of hunger, because when we travel he can wait an hour or two before eating breakfast. Only after he told me about living in the woods of Latvia and hiding from the Germans during World War II did I understand. The refugees often had only a hunk of stale bread to eat all day long. Many days there was nothing. Unconsciously, my husband is warding off a day's starvation by eating dry toast each morning. Hunger and bread made an impression on the child that has manifested itself into a lifelong adult habit. That is memoir.

Now that you understand memoir, and if you've decided to write yours, here are four points to help you perfect your project:

1. Be original

There are certain subjects that have been done over and over. A memoir doesn't need to involve child abuse, rape or murder to grab a reader's attention. Try to find small stories with interesting details or twists that your readers could imagine happening to them. They will identify with your struggle, your laughter and your tears, even if their own experience was nothing like yours.

2. Supplement your memory

Visit old places, your old neighborhood, your work place, and talk to the people who were involved with your past. Always double-check your historical facts for accuracy. Nothing ruins a writer's credibility more than placing a product in your setting before it was invented, or positioning the old schoolhouse on a street that has always been a landfill.

3. Focus on your point

Not your point of view, which is obviously first person, but decide whether you wish to tell a humorous story or a tragic one. Do you look at life as an eternal lesson from which you are constantly learning, or was there tragedy that has shaped your life in a way you have only recently come to recognize?

Sergeant Friday's "Just the facts, Ma'am" doesn't apply to writing the memoir. You must tell your own version of what happened through your personal and emotionally colored lens. The facts alone may be interesting, but for readers to relive the story with you, you must draw them into your emotions.

Inherent in your decision will be the consideration of the other people in your story. Are they still alive? What will be their reaction to your story? How will that influence your writing? Do you wish to discuss their appearance in your story with them ahead of time?

4. Decide where to begin your story

Certainly not on the day you were born, unless there was something of significance in that day or event, other than your own arrival. As in good fiction, begin with a conflict, internal or external. Homer H. Hickam, Jr., the author of *Rocket Boys: A Memoir*, advises the writer to set parallel plots, as in a novel. His successful memoir not only carried the main thread of rocket-building, but it interwove three additional threads about his love interest, his family and his town.

It is a good idea to follow a chronological time sequence as much as possible. Because it is a story based on memories, the reader can become easily confused by jumping forward and back in time.

Writing a memoir can be a rewarding experience for the writer and, in many cases such as my husband's, a healing one. Start taking notes on your memories, practice a little psychology and ask yourself why you do things in that certain way. Listen to your feelings when you hear an old song. You may have the material for an entertaining or inspiring memoir resting in your own memory.

McCourt, Frank. *Angela's Ashes: A Memoir*. Touchstone Books, 1999, ISBN: 068484267X

Benson, Vincent and Benson, Victoria. *To No Man's Glory: A Child's Journey From Holocaust To Healing*. Silver Dove Publishing Co., 2000, ISBN: 0967656605

McDonnell, Jane Taylor. *Living To Tell The Tale: A Guide To Writing Memoir*. Penguin USA, 1998, ISBN: 0140265309

Hickam, Homer H., Jr. *Rocket Boys: A Memoir*. Delacorte Press, 1998, ISBN: 0385333218

*For historical writers, the
tracing paper is an essential
piece of equipment.*

Time Off For Good Behavior

by Peggy Ullman Bell

Y ou've diligently worked your fingers, and your brain, for fifty weeks, and now it's time to rest. You've packed your leisure duds, camera, scuba gear, hiking boots, bicycling togs, whatever, and you're ready to take off.

Did you unplug the computer? A surge protector protects for only one surge and you aren't going to be around to put in a new fuse. Did you pack all essential gear? Are you sure?

How about those pocket note pads? Plenty of pens? Charcoal? A sketch pad? Tracing paper? Hey! This is a vacation!

Fortunately, or unfortunately (depending on your point of view), your mind does not go on vacation. Your memory does, however—and often. Every experience writers have is grist for their personal story mill. No photograph can capture the *feel* of sunrise over Nantucket or the sunset over Catalina. You cannot photograph the whispers of the gods that may come to you within the cloud-shroud on top of Old Smokey, or the twitter of mermaids in the Costa Rican twilight.

Ghosts reside in most national parks. Can you hear them? Will you remember what they said on that distant day when you need them for your current story? That dilapidated cabin over there might be a perfect setting for a someday story, but, unless you make a rough sketch, unless you jot down your inner impressions, you will not be able to call it to mind.

Years from now, when you dust off a box from your attic and look at your "essential" vacation photos, how will you remember exactly why you took them if you don't have notes copied on the back of them after they're processed?

Okay—now you have the hang of it. "But why tracing paper?" you may say.

For historical writers, the tracing paper is an essential piece of equipment. Natural historians, and that is what most of us are, spend a lot of time prowling around old cemeteries and museums—vacation or no. There will come a time when your tracings of interesting epitaphs and monument inscriptions will be invaluable to you.

You simply cannot catch the essence of an old tombstone by jotting down the epitaph. The style of lettering alone may provide needed inspiration for a story. A reproduction of a tracing may be what sells an editor on your story. Something is lacking in "Here lies Jim Smith. He called Joe Barnes a liar." It loses its punch without the crooked, hand-carved, misspelled lettering.

The uniqueness of the inscription on a nineteenth-century monument, in sometown, south somewhere, does not come across without the endlessly curled letters and the minute, carved art of the original. And a twenty-first century photograph will not do justice to its heights and shadows. For that, you need charcoal and tracing paper.

Now that I've turned your vacation into work, I'll take mine—right here at my keyboard—working for travel money so I can soon follow my own advice.

Mystery

Other aspects of character come into play as you contemplate tools for murder.

Choosing a Murder Weapon

by Marcia Kiser

R emember the game Clue™ and Colonel Mustard in the conservatory with Miss Scarlett—er, I mean, with the lead pipe? Remember how much fun it was trying to determine "whodunit" and with what?

If you think about it, Clue™ is a classic cozy mystery boiled down to bare essentials: six suspects, nine rooms, and six weapons. Oh, and what lovely weapons they are: the knife, the candlestick, the revolver, the rope, the lead pipe, and the wrench. A charming assortment of homicidal instruments. The only thing missing from this almost complete list of classics is Dame Agatha's weapon of choice: poison.

In the past few months, I've read mysteries with a surprising array of murder weapons—a Japanese sword, an IV of medication used to put animals to sleep, a rare neurotoxin from fish, carbon monoxide poisoning, drug and alcohol overdose, food poisoning (selective, of course), not to mention the classic blunt instrument, and the more mundane guns and knives. In one of my own novels, I use stampeding cattle as the murder weapon. (A little unusual, I admit, but when in Texas...)

So, how do you choose, from the vast array of weapons available, the perfect murder weapon for your killer to use?

There are two major considerations: the killer and the crime.

Let's look at killers first. Not every killer would be comfortable with the lethal force of a gun, knife or blunt instrument. At the same time, not everyone would be comfortable with the subtleties of poison. Does your killer have an area of expertise? Is there something in her/his background that could determine the use of an unexpected weapon?

An avid gardener is familiar with insecticides and all sorts of chemicals. The gardener might be familiar with certain varieties of toxic plants that each of us grows in our backyard garden. Also, the gardener might be familiar enough with insects to make our six-legged friends a viable murder weapon. People allergic to bee stings and other insect venom always carry medication to prevent anaphylactic shock. A clever murderer could withhold the emergency kit, and the death could be ruled accidental.

Or is your killer a big, bluff, good ol' boy redneck? It is doubtful that a good ol' boy would use poison. Thinking stereotypically, you may first imagine that his personality screams for lethal force. You can easily see him using a double-barreled shotgun. But consider for a moment: what if the good ol' boy once worked for a commercial hothouse and knows all about the harmful effects of insecticides? Wouldn't that lend unexpected interest to the mystery?

Other aspects of character come into play as you contemplate tools for murder. A less subtle person would most likely choose a blunt instrument, a gun or a knife—with more immediate results (but not necessarily less violent) than with poisoning. I've read repeatedly over the years that women use poison and blunt instruments more than men do and that men tend to use guns and knives. I don't know whether this observation is true, but it may help decide what weapon to choose.

Conversely, timid people might also choose a gun—allowing more distance between them and their victim so that they can keep their hands clean, in a sense.

A professional killer (one who's for hire) might use anything from garroting to a car bomb to physical torture, without feeling any emotion at all. Assassins are, after all, paid to kill people whom they usually don't know. The weapon choice is usually a matter of expedience.

So, whether the killer is a Jane Marple look-alike or bears a strong resemblance to Hannibal (the cannibal) Lectern, personality will give the best clues to the right weapon to use.

Next, look at the crime. Is it spur of the moment? Could your killer be a quiet person finally pushed beyond the boundaries of civilization? Is the murder a crime of passion? Or could it possibly be accidental? A hard shove, a stumble, and the victim's head hits a large stone or a piece of furniture.

In the heat of the moment, a blunt instrument, or perhaps a gun or a knife, would most likely be used. Your killer will grab whatever happens to be readily available when he or she is so enraged that all sense of right and wrong is lost and the only consideration is to stop the other person.

In this case, a hard shove is a good weapon—especially if the scene is set with a staircase, concrete steps, a coffee table, or something similar. A simple shove into any of these objects will almost assuredly result in death if the blow lands in the correct area. Of course, a quick shove off a mountain or a cliff face leaves little room for doubt.

A crime of passion certainly doesn't lend itself to pre-planning, but the killer's covering up the crime can give the writer lots of room to work, layering clues and motives.

Premeditation, on the other hand, by definition, allows for plenty of time to "set the scene." The killer can bring the weapon of choice to the murder scene. Or the killer can set the murder scene in advance: tying fishing line across the top step of a dimly lit staircase; substituting some type of lethal medication inside an innocent cold capsule; replacing certain household cleaners with other, more lethal, liquids so the fumes do the work. With a little research and some careful planning, we can use almost anything we touch as a murder weapon. A chilling thought, isn't it?

Where weapon choice is concerned, the sky is definitely the limit. Research your chosen weapon. If you use a gun, find a target range that rents guns and try one out. Make sure you don't confuse an automatic with a revolver.

If you use a knife, find a self-defense instructor who can show you how the knife should be held and what kinds of "defense wounds" the victim would have as a result of the struggle. Check with an emergency room doctor or a trauma team or the local coroner to determine where the knife should enter the body— you don't want the knife to be deflected by bone.

With a little time and effort, and with some help from your character, the perfect murder weapon is out there, just waiting to be discovered. Happy hunting!

The Mystery Genre And Its Offspring

by Sunnye Tiedemann

The murder or the heist are not what matters in the mystery novel. Paramount is the solution and the way that solution is discovered or devised. A crime is committed and the quest is on—it is cerebral, challenging, sporting. The game's the thing. Whether the means justifies the end becomes the abiding question as the story progresses.

"Readers of detective novels," writes David Lehman in *The Perfect Murder*, "participate in perfect murders—perfect because they offer us a vicarious and therefore socially acceptable form of releasing our homicidal instincts, and they allow us to do it again and again and again, letting us off the hook each time, without having to face the consequences." It is also true that readers of detective novels in the safety and comfort of their reading chair relish reckless adventures that they most certainly would not enjoy in the least had they encountered them personally.

The mystery novel as we know it began 150 years ago as a short story. Edgar Allen Poe is generally regarded as the initial American mystery writer, with his still-stunning, "Murders in the Rue Morgue," the classic locked-room mystery. The genre has since grown and expanded through a number of transformations—from story to novel to movie—spawning a variety of major subgenres: private detective (or P.I.), the cozy (otherwise known as the traditional mystery), amateur detective, suspense novel, police procedural, romantic suspense, thriller, puzzle, and the historical suspense, all of which continue to thrive, to evolve and to grow in popularity.

These varied subgenres all have three elements in common: a crime (and it need not be murder), a villain or perpetrator (otherwise known as "the perp"), and the person who solves the crime. The all-encompassing questions of any mystery are who committed the offense, how, and why.

The mystery presents a problem of life-and-death importance, challenging a slightly better-than-average hero or heroine, whose behavior throughout the book demonstrates resourcefulness and intelligence in solving the problem. The construction of a mystery is unique in that the narrative line flows upstream, as it were, from effect to cause, so that the reader must follow the action closely and must guess at the meaning of events as he or she interprets a variety of clues. Novelists in the genre rely heavily on constructing tight plots involving suspense, surprise, reversals, and recognitions.

The subgenres of mystery often seem to blend into each other. Agatha Christie's Miss Marple, for example, is an amateur detective, and her stories' settings and style are very much those of a cozy. To further confuse the genre issue, it must be noted that, in one sense, all mysteries are puzzles, since all involve a protagonist who must mentally fit the pieces together. The puzzle mystery per se, however, has certain characteristics that distinguish it from other categories.

Puzzle mysteries are based on a gimmick. The gimmick is involved some way in the commission of the murder, and, as events unfold, that same gimmick points to the perpetrator and the resolution of the problem. The solution depends on the inductive (and deductive) powers of the protagonist in interpreting clues. Erle Stanley Gardner, in his Perry Mason series, and John Dickson Carr, who wrote locked-room mysteries, excelled at these.

The private investigator (or P. I.) main character is a hard-livin', fast-talkin', wenching, hard-boiled, all-American tough guy. This hero, personified by Dashiell Hammett's Sam Spade, Raymond Chandler's Phillip Marlow, Mickey Spillane's Mike Hammer, John D. MacDonald's Travis McGee, and Robert B. Parker's Spenser, is a loner, high-principled and honorable, suspicious of women but available. He often has a long-suffering female hovering nearby who looks after him and eats her little heart out in unrequited love. The P. I. stereotype began as a parody, evolved into a style, and has recently developed a distaff side, thanks to Sara Paretsky's V. I. Warshawski and Sue Grafton's Kinsey Milhone. The P. I. subgenre has come a long way, baby, but whether it's a he or a she, the private investigator charges full-steam ahead, wisecracking all the way to the solution.

The amateur detective (featured in the traditional or "cozy" mysteries), is sometimes classified as a subgenre of the P. I. She or he is usually independently wealthy, or at least is independent of the need to earn money. She/he is also appropriately endowed with unusual intellectual powers, the better to analyze when facts need correlating. Amateurs don't use weapons or nasty language. They don't encounter violence (except after the fact), raw sex, blood, or gore. Doyle's Sherlock Holmes, Chesterton's Father Brown, Sayers's Peter Wimsey, and Christie's Hercule Poirot and Jane Marple all fit this category. Modern amateur sleuths abound by the dozens and include Carolyn Hart's Annie Darling, Elizabeth Peters's Amelia Peabody Emerson and Nancy Picard's Jenny Cain.

The Police Procedural came along in the forties. In these stories, the sleuth relies on professional techniques and scientific methods of police and/or coroner investigations to solve the crime. Lawrence Treat is credited with the first example of this subgenre; renditions by Hillary Waugh, Ed McBain, Colin Dexter, and others closely followed.

Charlotte Bronte, with *Jane Eyre*, gets credit for being the procreator of romantic suspense, but few have succeeded in this genre better than Daphne du Maurier, who penned the unforgettable Rebecca.

Generally, books in this subgenre feature the heroine in some sort of danger, either physical or psychological. The protagonist is beautiful and resourceful; the hero, handsome and successful; the villain, resourceful and evil. In the classic romantic suspense story, there is immediate sexual attraction between the hero and heroine when they meet, and the rest of the story combines eroticism with danger and wickedness. Modern authors have changed the procedure a bit but not to the detriment of the type. Look for books by Mary Higgins Clark (*The Lottery Winner, Silent Night,* and *Let Me Call You Sweetheart*), Alice Hoffman (*Turtle Moon*), and Barbara Victor (*Coriander*).

Thrillers (spy-thrillers or techno-thrillers) are filled with international intrigue and danger, and the action moves between continents. The good country fights the bad, and technology runs rampant. Plots hinge on the fight to save a country, a way of life, or an international corporation. David Cornwell, John Le Carre, Tom Clancy, and Ken Follett are authors who have succeeded in writing best-selling thrillers.

Lately, historical mysteries are everywhere. These may be built around famous people from the past, such as Eleanor Roosevelt in Elliott Roosevelt's series; Agatha Christie and Dorothy Sayers in Gaylord Larson's *Agatha and*

Dorothy; and Peter Sayer's Bertie series, featuring King Edward VII as sleuth. Or, an author may simply take a historical happening or event as setting or premise for murder, as do Loren Estleman in *Edsel* and Robert Barnard in *Dead, Mr. Mozart*.

There are other subgenres—caper novels and those with serial killers, novels of psychological menace, science-fiction mysteries, adventure-action mysteries, and cute-couple mysteries (who could forget Nick and Nora Charles or Mr. and Mrs. North?).

Their number is legion and their fans devoted.

"The first job of the detective novelist," writes Lehman, "is to convince us that our lives are not as drab and humdrum as we fear, that menace lurks under every surface and conspiracy is in the air, that we've a perfect right to be paranoid." There is no greater challenge to a writer than to craft a well-constructed, fast-moving, reader-gripping mystery novel; there is no greater delight to a mystery reader than to discover one.

Lehman, David. *The Perfect Murder.* Free Press, 1998, ASIN: 0029197708

Short Story

*There are as many credible ways to
write stories as there are people
writing them.*

How To Write A Short Story

by Sunnye Tiedemann

Here's a look at several methods for writing a contemporary short story. Unless you are exceptionally talented and have unusually good instincts, you'll have to do a little bit of studying and a lot of practicing before you produce a commercially publishable story. Then, if you're lucky, you'll find an editor who will take the time and have the patience to fine-tune your skills.

So what is a short story? One way to a definition is to say what something isn't: It isn't a vignette. It isn't a "moment in time." It isn't something that happened, although events can be translated into short stories.

The contemporary commercial short story (at least a publishable one) has a beginning, a middle, and an end. It is about change. Something happens to the main character that results in an epiphany and changes him or her at the end. An exception is the mystery, where the change begins the story and the rest of the tale is about correcting a wrong and making things right again.

One caveat: Do not wait for inspiration. Like genius, stories are 2% inspiration and 98% perspiration. Apply your fingers to the keyboard and write.

Any short story is about a character, so begin with your protagonist. Think of two people you admire, and make a list of the things you like most about them. Then list the things you like least. If you can't think of anything negative about a person, think of someone you don't like, and list what you don't like most about him or her. Now, actually, you have two characters.

Develop story people your readers can identify with. (An excellent source for learning how to create credible characters is *Creating Characters: How To Build Story People* by Dwight Swain.)

Take four characteristics you do like and one you don't, and build your protagonist around these.

Now take two characteristics you like and two you don't, and build your antagonist around those.

If you're writing a murder mystery, the first thing you do is kill off a "significant other" of the protagonist's or a person who is otherwise closely connected in some way. If you are writing straight fiction, have something happen to the main character that he can't control, or have him go after something he wants.

The difference between mystery and other fiction is significant: In mystery fiction, the protagonist begins with the crisis and proceeds from there. In most mysteries, the process doesn't significantly change the character. In other contemporary fiction, however, the protagonist encounters events that lead to a crisis, which in turn produces an epiphany that changes him or her forever.

Now set the antagonist against your protagonist, and every time your heroine makes a move, pit the villain against her. Have your heroine struggle to make things come out right, but make the results of that struggle unexpected so that things come out all wrong. As one Hollywood producer said, "Put him up and tree and shoot at him."

There are as many credible ways to write stories as there are people writing them. If you've a story in mind, the best thing to do is to write it out. Let the story decide its length. "Stories are never written," a famous writer once said. "They are always rewritten." Get the tale told. Then comes the fun part: the rewrite.

If there is a secret to writing publishable short stories, it is this: Construct the story in a series of scenes. If you are writing scenes and sequels, you are "showing" rather than "telling."

Each scene must evolve from the one before. One of the best books about this method is Jack Bickham's *Writing Novels That Sell*. In it, the revered author and teacher of many authors describes the technique of scene and sequel and demonstrates it. Bickham's book *Writing The Short Story* is another superb reference for aspiring writers.

In your first rewrite, work on the beginning. This should be the moment that changes everything and begins the inevitable march toward the crisis. The first sentence should be something memorable. Set up the situation through the eyes of the character who is most affected by it. Then, as you write, insert the background of the story and characters as subtly as you can, revealing the information in dialogue and small bits of narrative. There's not much room for flashbacks in a short story, those are best saved for novels.

As you finish a scene, ask your protagonist, "What happens next?" It's the perennial question of fiction, and only the characters can answer it.

In short stories, it's best to keep the character count to a minimum so as not to confuse the reader. Make names distinct so that they are not easily confused. If Mary is in the story you're writing now, save Marie for the next one.

As you work your way through the middle of the story, build suspense. Suspense keeps your reader turning the page. When you reach the crisis, you're ready to begin the ending.

Make the ending dramatic, tense, final, and swift.

There are a number of important details you will have included because they're indispensable. Place, for one example; mood, for another. Voice, point of view— all these considerations need to be taken into account when you rewrite. It's usually easier to do a rewrite for each detail rather than try to think of everything at once. Make a pass just to check point of view, for instance, and then go over the piece again, this time checking to be sure that the setting is consistent with events of the story.

There are so many things to consider that you may wonder how Hemingway ever had time to worry over each individual word. You'll find with practice that more of these things will become automatic and need less fixing in the rewrites.

Have your story critiqued by another writer. Not by your Mom or next door neighbor or husband, but by someone who knows about the process and, if you can find them, by people who know the publishing industry.

So there you are, your own short story. Send it out, forget about it, and begin another.

Swain, Dwight. *Creating Characters: How To Build Story People*. Writers Digest Books, 1994 (reprint), ISBN: 0898796628

Bickham, Jack. *Writing Novels That Sell*. Fireside, 1989, ASIN: 0671683934

Bickham, Jack. *Writing the Short Story*. Writers Digest Books, 1994, ASIN: 0898796709

Because the reader needs to feel immediate
compassion for the main character,
characterization is more important
than the plot.

How To Write The Confession Story

by Rose P. Lee

*T*he major confession magazines began in the days of the pulp magazines. Their audience was the working class female between the ages of
eighteen and twenty-five. Titles were crafted to lure women to buy magazines that contained scandalous (for those times) stories. At the time, the
young working woman had few magazine choices. She could not identify
with the expensive ads in the "glossies," and their stories made her feel like
a failure in life.

Confession stories were about females from broken homes who made
bad choices, married young, and soon had a baby. The only type of employment available to them was the low-level, low-paying job, much like the job
the magazine reader was likely to hold. After a hard day of being on her feet
in a 5 & 10 cent store, factory, or diner, a young working woman wanted to
soak her feet, grab a can of soda or beer, turn on the radio, and read about
other women similar to herself. The confession stories filled the need and
were inexpensive, as well.

The stories were formulaic. Typically, a girl's father died, and her un-
educated mother could not support the family. Deprived of a structured
home life, the young woman did not finish high school, chose the "wild"
boy, suffered a calamity, and then finished her GED or attended beauty
school. The heroine then married the nice "dull boy," had children and
lived happily ever after. All stories were written in first person, all from the

confessor's point of view, and most contained the love triangle of two boys (one good and one bad) and the main character. Usually, confession magazines are not sexually graphic.

Since confession stories have always been anonymous, no one will ever know how many of today's writers both earned money and learned their craft by writing confession stories. The stories are supposedly true, so there is never a byline. Most beginning writers prefer to see their names in print, but they also realize the value of not having a history as a confession writer.

If you wish to write successfully for today's confession market, start by buying and reading all the confession magazines you can for a three-month period, to discover which one suits your style and interest. (Be sure the editor is the same for all three issues.)

Most stories are based upon a small incident from which the writer develops a story. The title is the real hook for the reader (and the editor). Usually, it has little to do with the story per se and is for shock value only. The stories are always in first person and the setting (time, place, and mood) is established in the first three paragraphs. Some confession magazines prefer stories that begin with the main character speaking to herself/himself or to another (never to a mirror).

The plots are simple, but the writing is intended to generate an emotional response. Because the reader needs to feel immediate compassion for the main character, characterization is more important than the plot. Typically, the confessor reveals she has been obsessed with the need to feel loved (hence boyfriend, food, alcohol/drugs, sex). Then, at the end, she changes the focus to a worthwhile goal. The reader wants the main character to accomplish her goal and to live happily ever after. Of course, the days of the GED and beauty school as goals are gone. Now the female main characters attend community college, work in offices, are travel agents or computer workers (never higher than supervisor), and may even aspire to a college degree. However, the primary goals are still husband and children.

Several confession magazines now include one male-point-of-view story per issue. When the main character is a male, he is either a blue or white-collar worker. Most male confessors have some college and are finishing school at night. The male main character never has a jail record. He is definitely a good guy, and his goals include more than career advancement. He always is or becomes a compassionate man, worthy of reader sympathy.

In current confession stories, the female main character has a middle-class goal, but a wild male keeps her from attaining her goal at first. She realizes her mistake and marries the nice guy who has been patiently waiting for her to "come to her senses." Their strong love, goals for a middle-class life, and love of children will make them happy for the rest of their lives.

Each confession has its own set of themes. Popular ones for female confessors include obsessive behavior, eating disorders, rape (relative, clergyman, step-father, boyfriend of her best friend), jail/prison, the runaway teen, phone sex, teenage prostitution, robbery for her boyfriend (he has a long police record and if caught would serve a long prison sentence—she has no record), cancer or some other deadly disease, and natural disasters (forest fire, flood, hurricane, or tornado).

Male-point-of-view stories have many similar themes but must include evidence of compassion. Examples are: a handy man who does chores for a woman living in substandard housing, or who babysits for a girl friend while she attends an evening community college class or volunteers for a church or community group.

There are definite changes in the range of stories sought by today's editors. Years ago, an editor might include as a main character an older woman who seemed a neighborhood nuisance, but who in the end assisted the heroine in accomplishing her goal. Today editors prefer to include one story per issue of an older woman who discovers dating again, decides to complete her high school or junior college diploma, and finds her "high school first love" who is now a widower, and marries him. The older woman has goals, changes her dowdy widow's clothing for new fashionable clothes and even colors her hair. Her adult children rarely approve of her new lifestyle, but the older-woman heroine is strong in her new beliefs and lifestyle.

Editors are also interested in stories with a disabled main character (male or female). The male handicapped person is active, enjoys sports, builds playground equipment for the community and assists the female character in developing her self-esteem. The female disabled character may feel sorry for herself initially, but then she meets a challenge and overcomes it. Sometimes she wins the heart of the good guy after recognizing how the bad guy had held her back from finding happiness.

Not all confession magazines are listed in *Writer's Market,* so it is important for interested writers to read all the magazines, then send for writer's guidelines to the publications that interest him or her. Each magazine has a different readership and writers must adhere strictly to the guidelines for each publication.

Confession editors move from one confession publication to another and then on to other publications. They tend to take their stable of reliable writers with them. Editors are loyal. They know each other, party together, and talk about their writers. Most editors hold an English degree, have college friends in publishing (for both magazines and books), and will recommend a particular writer who performs well consistently. Confession editors operate as a clique and the writers they favor are those who adhere to professional standards. Do not assume that, because confession readers may not be highly educated, the manuscript can be submitted with poor grammar and incorrect spelling.

The confession magazine market pays little (just as when it started), but it is a place to hone one's writing skills and become known by editors. It offers a beginning, with editors who will work with new authors, recognize skill and effort, and reward dependable writers with contracts.

Creative Nonfiction

Just the facts, Ma'am
Why Joe Friday Could Never Write Creative Nonfiction

by Rodney Lewis Merrill

When I was in junior high school, *Dragnet* was a popular television show. Its somewhat jaded main character was investigative interlocutor Joe Friday. Friday was a low-key, no-nonsense kind of guy who had a knack for running into long-winded, curler-festooned witnesses who wanted to tell him about the victim's cousin's neighbor's dog. Friday would listen, stone-faced, for a while, then the lips on his expressionless face would part ever-so-slightly. Experienced *Dragnet* viewers adopted Friday's deadpan expression at that point and droned in unison with him: "Just the facts, Ma'am."

"Just the facts, Ma'am" became a household, workplace, and schoolyard expression. It was a cute way to say, "Get to the point."

But you know what? I'd hate to read *In Cold Blood* if Joe Friday had written it rather than Truman Capote. It would be dull. Even the potentially gory details would be dull. And, the truth is, finding a corpse, weapon, and killer do not constitute *the facts* of the case. What Joe Friday could never understand is that the *facts* in the case depend on who you are and where you are standing within the social and physical milieu.

Over one hundred years ago, painter Paul Cezanne came to this realization about *facts* while he sat at an easel and watched the appearance of his subject change more quickly than he could paint it. The light changed. The relative position of the subject to other objects changed. He noticed that the subject changed when his own eyes shifted, even infinitesimally. In other words, his subject appeared to change whenever the environment changed or when the observer changed. Cezanne concluded that art cannot report "reality" or "the facts"—it must represent the interaction between the see-ing and the being.

Around the same time, physicist Werner Heisenberg began to suspect that even "scientific observation" is subject to "the uncertainty principle"—the notion that all observation is skewed by the means of observing, the time of observing, and the idiosyncratic subjectivity of the observer. This being true, no scientific observation is truly reproducible; nor can it be said to yield a singular and objective truth. Scientific "facts" are more or less deductions derived by generalizing the intersections of observation and ig-noring the divergences.

This "paradigm shift" gradually overtook many fields of theory and practice. Writers, though, maintained the sharp distinction between cre-ative, imaginative writing—fiction—and the more or less plodding factual writing called "nonfiction" and "journalism." It wasn't until the 1960s and 1970s that Gay Talese, Thomas Wolfe, and Truman Capote crossed the sacrosanct line between fiction and nonfiction by adapting fictional tech-niques to "the facts."

I like to use Truman Capote and his famous *In Cold Blood* along side Joe Friday because *In Cold Blood* is about a murder. Whereas Joe Friday's "facts" boiled down to a weapon, a corpse, and a killer, Truman Capote's facts filled a large volume. Capote resurrected the corpses for a few hours and returned them to the living and the loved. He placed them in their environment—to the best of his understanding—by employing the fiction techniques of scene-building, dialogue, and description. In other words, he allowed them to be real to us in a way that an unknown corpse-victim cannot be real. In the same way, he allowed the murderers to be tangible and fleshy to us in a way that unknown assailants cannot. He allowed the situation to be far more horrible than "the facts" could possibly allow—as horrible as it really was.

Old school nonfiction writers still decry this process, saying, "How could Truman Capote know all this? How could he toy with 'the facts' like that? He's making it up. It's all a lie and a fraud." But new-school writers—"liter-ary journalists" and "creative nonfiction" writers like me—believe that to tell the truth about a situation, you immerse yourself in what is known. You talk to people who knew all the subjects involved. You dig through personal and public papers. You talk.

In the case of Truman Capote's *In Cold Blood*, this meant talking with everyone who knew the victims and the killers, and collecting everything that might reveal something, anything, about them. Capote used all "the facts" available to him to understand his subjects, their history, their influences, their way of talking, their way of thinking, and their way of behaving—normally and under stress. He embellished "the facts" with intimate, detailed description. He placed the facts within one or more points of view. In short, he built, with strict veracity, a larger context within which the reader could stand and come to understand the facts and to feel about them as he did.

Old-school journalists would have you say, "Three bodies—apparently father, mother, and daughter—were found in a farmhouse. They appeared to have been bound, gagged, then killed. Two men were convicted of the killings. There was no apparent motive."

Modern nonfiction writers say, as Cezanne said of painting, that modern writing cannot report on "reality" or "the facts" without representing the interaction between the seeing and the being.

Truman Capote *In Cold Blood*. Vintage Books, 1994 (reprint),
ISBN: 0679745580

Writing The Little Gem

by Sunnye Tiedemann

*H*enry Irving was telling a story to Mark Twain. He'd just begun the tale when he suddenly stopped and said, "You haven't heard this one, have you?" Twain assured him he had not. A little later Irving paused and asked the same question. Twain gave the same answer. When Irving got to the climax of the story, he broke off again saying, "Are you quite sure you haven't heard this?" The third time was too much for Twain. "I can lie once," Twain said, "I can lie twice for courtesy's sake, but I draw the line there. I can't lie the third time at any price. I not only heard the story, I invented it."

As artists often add small dabs of color to brighten a canvas, so authors add anecdotes to their nonfiction articles and manuscripts to strengthen a point or to emphasize a theme. An anecdote is a mini-story based on an event. It's a single incident that, like a short story, has a beginning, a middle, and an end. In the anecdote there is no character development and, usually, no setting.

An anecdote is a great way to hook a reader at the very beginning of an article. It's also a fine way to make a memorable ending. It can take dull material and liven it up, much as a dash of salt brings out flavor in a vegetable. A short illustration can drive home a point, can change the pace of a piece, or can provide insight into a theme. In short, careful use of anecdotal illustrations in your articles can make the difference between a piece that sells and one that gets you a flock of rejections.

That's what an anecdote is. Now let's look at when to use it, how to use it, and how to write it. And yes, it is all right to make up anecdotes to emphasize a point in your article.

Whether you use an anecdotal illustration in your manuscript and how much you use it depends on the kind of article you're writing and the length of the piece. Each anecdote must illustrate the point you are making. The story may be tailored to fit, you may even alter quotations, but the truth of the story must be kept intact, and it must be appropriate.

There are three parts to this kind of story. First, there's the set-up. The first sentence or two introduces the characters and sets up the problem or situation. The middle sentences amplify the situation, wasting no time on extraneous details. The last sentences close the story with a satisfying ending.

When you write an anecdote, you tell events in sequence. There's no place for flashbacks or backstory in the short illustration. It is told quickly and simply.

— Do not include extra information—this is no time to worry about setting or characterization.

— Do not explain, or if you must, keep your explanation simple and use description sparingly.

— Use dialogue. The strongest anecdotes are quick glimpses of life, and strong, appropriate use of dialogue lends a sense of reality to a story.

You may wonder where you can find anecdotes for articles. In a sense, they are all around you. They are in the conversations you overhear in public places, and in social discourse you share with friends and acquaintances. They're in your own experience, in your past and present and future. You'll find them in stories and articles, in brochures and in public relations handouts. You can even make them up, beginning with an appropriate quotation or an incident that would serve to illustrate a point. In short, you can't beat an anecdote for strengthening your articles and adding interest and color.

*Synoptic openings get to the
point. Ironically, though, they
make for slower reading than
dramatic depiction.*

It Was A Dark And Stormy Night:
Writing the Opening

by Rodney Lewis Merrill

*I*n *Right Ho, Jeeves*, Bertie Wooster says of writing an opening: "I don't
know if you've had the same experience, but the snag I always come up
against when I'm telling a story is this dashed difficult problem of where
to begin it. It's a thing you don't want to go wrong over, because one false
step and you're sunk. I mean, if you fool about too long at the start, trying
to establish atmosphere, as they call it, and all that sort of rot, you fail to
grip and the customers walk out on you."

Just so.

What makes the literary journalist (the creative nonfiction writer) different from a newspaper reporter is that he or she is intent on telling a story.
Consequently, the literary journalist has to make many of the same choices
made by writers of invented (fictional) stories. Who will tell the story? The
author? The subject(s)? Interviewees? More often than not, the decision is
determined by the author's comfort with person and point of view, and by
his or her sense of which mode suits the particular story.

Like the fiction writer, like Bertie Wooster, the literary journalist wants
to "grip" the customers before they walk out. The most important decision,
aside from who will tell the story and what will be the point of view, *is* the
storytelling modality you want to use for the opening. Openings tend to be
synoptic or dramatic.

A synoptic opening telescopes information that spans more time and
detail than the average attention span could tolerate in a verbatim rendition

of events. It tells the reader in a few sentences a quantity of information that might require dozens of pages if rendered in detail. And that is its strength. Synoptic openings get to the point. Ironically, though, they make for slower reading than dramatic depiction. Even though it quickly bridges large spans of time and detail, summation evokes an impression of "second-handedness" that reduces reader involvement and creates a sense of lumbering pace.

Don't believe it? Go back and read the opening to this article, then re-read the preceding paragraph. They contain the same number of words. (I allow, of course, that some narrative paragraphs are more alluring than others.)

In Dicken's day, readers didn't mind a lumbering introduction. Life was slower paced. Readers were willing to broach a book slowly, to allow the author the opportunity to properly introduce him/herself and to announce his/her intentions. They were willing to enter a story as one might inch one's way into the water, taking time to acclimate body and soul to the task. They felt no compulsion to dive in headlong into the deep end. Long and, it now seems, painfully drawn out openings were commonplace.

I don't want to leave you with the impression that all synoptic openings are tedious. Some literary journalists are extremely talented in narration, and their facility with it compensates for its innate liabilities. Just look at this synoptic opening to Truman Capote's *In Cold Blood*:

> "Until one morning in mid-November of 1959, few Americans, in fact, few Kansans, had ever heard of Holcomb. Like the waters of the river, like the motorists on the highway, and like the yellow trains streaking down the Santa Fe tracks, drama, in the shape of exceptional happenings, had never stopped there. The inhabitants of the village, numbering two hundred and seventy, were satisfied that this should be so, quite content to exist inside ordinary life, to work, to hunt, to watch television, to attend school socials, choir practice, meetings of the 4H Club. But then, in the earliest hours of the morning in November, a Sunday morning, certain foreign sounds impinged on the normal nightly Holcomb noises—on the keening hysteria of coyotes, the dry scrape of scuttling tumbleweed, the racing, receding wail of locomotive whistles. At the time not a soul in sleeping Holcomb heard them—four shotgun blasts that, all told, ended six human lives. But afterward the townspeople,

thereto sufficiently unfearful of each other to seldom trouble to lock their doors, found fantasy re-creating them over and again, those somber explosions that stimulates fires of mistrust in the glare of which many old neighbors viewed each other strangely, and as strangers."

Cool! Two hundred and three well-chosen words. One of the best synoptic openings written, and certainly as intriguing as any piece of fiction on the same subject. And notice that it relies on images. A well-written synoptic narrative opening does that: it conjures up vivid images that, even in the absence of dialogue and drama, beguile its readers long enough for the author to forge within them a yen to know more.

Still, the frazzled readers of today, weaned as they are on remote-controlled MTV, picture-within-a picture, and MP3 technology, want action. They want movement. And nothing spells action and movement like a dramatic scene and/or dialogue. Without mincing words, it throws readers into the water, no matter how cold or deep. (A side note: psychologists say we learn and remember things that involve us much better than we remember things simply told to us.)

In fiction, one of my favorite dramatic openings of this type is this opening-with-attitude from J.D. Salinger's *The Catcher In The Rye*:

> If you really want to hear about it, the first thing you'll probably want to know is where I was born, and what my lousy childhood was like, and how my parents were occupied and all before they had me, and all that David Copperfield kind of crap, but I don't feel like going into it, if you want to know the truth.

No lollygagging around for Salinger. Boom! You're there. Such an opening may seem less plausible with nonfiction, but Hunter S. Thompson frequently pulls it off in his creative nonfiction. (To be sure, Hunter Thompson is an acquired taste, but that's another matter.)

Salinger opens in first person and from the protagonist's point of view, and stays with it through one walloping chapter after another. In contrast, Helene Hanff, in *84, Charing Cross Road*, maintains person while switching point of view through the clever use of postal correspondence. Yet her opening is just as immediate:

Gentlemen:

Your ad in the *Saturday Review Of Literature* says that you specialize in out-of-print books. The phrase "antiquarian booksellers" scares me somewhat, as I equate "antique" with expensive. I am a poor writer with antiquarian taste in books and all things I want are impossible to get over here except very expensive rare editions, or in Barnes & Noble's grimy, marked-up schoolboy copies.

I enclose a list of my most pressing problems. If you have clean secondhand copies of any of the books on the list, for no more than $5.00 each, will you consider this a purchase order and send them to me?

Very truly yours,

Helene Hanff [hand signed]"
(Miss) Helene Hanff

Okay, this isn't the head-slammer Salinger's Holden Caulfield gives us, but these 110 words tell you a great deal about Helene, the story she has to offer, and the timbre of its telling. If you don't like this opening, you won't like the book. (More's the pity, on both counts.)

Studs Terkel, a writer of creative nonfiction, can be depended upon to come up with a good opener In *Race*, Terkel opens with this:

> "It obsesses everybody," declaimed my impassioned friend, "even those who think they are not obsessed. My wife was driving down the street in a black neighborhood. The people at the corners were all gesticulating at her. She was very frightened, turned up the windows, and drove determinedly. She discovered, after several blocks, she was going the wrong way on a one way street and they were trying to help her. Mind you, she's a very enlightened person. You'd never associate her with racism, yet her first reaction was that they were dangerous."

Terkel uses the dramatic immediacy of anecdotal conversation to cover ground that might have consumed several rather arid pages of description.

Either opening method, synoptic or dramatic, is equally valid. Some literary journalists do their best to blend them in a single opening that takes advantage of the best each has to offer—descriptive imagery and dramatic immediacy—without fooling about so long, as Bertie Wooster put it, that you fail to "grip" and the customers walk out on you.

Wodehouse, P. G.. Life With Jeeves: The Inimitable Jeeves, Very Good, Jeeves!, and Right Ho, Jeeves. *Viking Press, 1993 (reprint), ISBN: 0140059024*

Capote, Truman, *In Cold Blood,* Vintage Books, 1994 (reprint), ISBN: 0679745580

Salinger, J.D.. *The Catcher In The Rye.* Little Brown & Company, 1951, ISBN: 0316769533

Hanff, Helene. *84, Charing Cross Road.* Penguin, 1990 (reissue), ISBN: 0140143505

Terkel, Studs. *Race.* Anchor, 1993, ISBN: 038546889X

Marketing

How well can you boil your story down to sixty words from sixty thousand?

Selling Your Novel in an Elevator

by Sheldon Reiffenstein

*I*n the penultimate scene of the movie *Working Girl,* corporate merger artist Jack Trainer leads the enterprising Tess McGill into an elevator where she can describe to a corporate tycoon how she came up with a brilliant entrepreneurial idea. She has a mere thirty seconds to convince the busy executive. She succeeds, turning herself from out-of-work secretary into ladder-climbing executive (and foiling the scheming rival who has claimed Tess's idea as her own).

Step back and contemplate what Tess accomplished in that elevator. Now, imagine you're in an elevator with the editor to whom you've been dying to present your manuscript. Do you think you could match Tess's success? Thirty seconds is about all the time you have to persuade an editor to ask for more. Can you boil your novel down to two or three button-pushing sentences? That's what you need to do when you're pitching your manuscript, whether face-to-face or through a query letter.

In the business world, salespeople are often faced with a prospect who doesn't know them, their products, or their company. The salesperson has to impress the prospect quickly to break through all the other clutter in the prospect's mind and get him to ask for more detail. What we in the sales-training business do is put people through an "Elevator Exercise." They pretend they're going from the ground floor to the twentieth, a thirty-second ride, with a prospect.

Their task is to persuade the prospect to agree to see and hear more about the product.

Your product is sixty or eighty thousand words. Your prospect is a person who has a few hundred aspiring authors pushing their manuscripts at her. She has thirty seconds to read your letter or listen to your pitch before she moves on to the next idea. How do you make your presentation good enough for her to ask for some chapters or even the whole manuscript? How well can you boil your story down to sixty words from sixty thousand? Are you able to sell your novel in an elevator?

It isn't that easy to boil down plots and subplots, character motivation, action, dialogue, and narrative into a few compelling statements. To help you along, we'll take an American classic, *Moby Dick*, as the novel for which we need to write our elevator pitch.

The first step is to write a single simple sentence about your story. Keep description bare, allowing yourself only the absolutely necessary words. Leave out adjectives and adverbs for now. A simple statement about *Moby Dick* is "A sailor goes fishing." That's bare bones and gives us a skeleton to build on. Why be so spare? The process is like building a model car. We start with the chassis alone. It's the foundation. If we were to try to put the doors or the windshield on at the beginning, they wouldn't fit and would get in the way of the frame. Our sentence is factual, doesn't bring any preconceived biases we have into the story line, and allows us to experiment with a variety of directions as we build the description.

Now let's add some detail. What does he go fishing for? In this story, the object of the venture is a whale—in fact, the largest whale in the ocean. The story line now reads, "A sailor goes fishing for a great white whale."

Next, let's add more information about the sailor. One could wonder about his motivation for this endeavor: what's his personal draw to this whale?

"An obsessed sea captain hunts a great white whale." Our statement is getting better. Notice that we've changed "fishing" to "hunts." "Hunt" is a stronger verb that implies motive. Also, we've indicated that he's obsessed and he's a captain. He has control over the crew, and his obsession could blind him to their safety. But what makes him obsessed? That question leads to the next version: "An obsessed sea captain, having lost a leg attempting to capture a great white whale, seeks to revenge his loss by hunting down the whale at all costs."

Now we have motive. Vengeance has always been an interesting motivator; here it is compelling since it is directed at a whale, not a person. However, a reader of this description may still feel a sense of "so what." You can almost hear the objections popping up in the editor's mind. "Whale hunting is not the type of activity that draws thousands of spectators. And isn't this peg-leg thing a bit clichéd?"

Okay, so the pitch isn't perfect—yet. Let's give it some body; let's show the futility of seeking revenge; how strong, misguided emotion blinds people; the tragic consequences of arrogance when men believe they can dominate nature. Here's the final summary. "In *Moby Dick*, Captain Ahab's obsession with killing the great whale sets him and his ship on a suicidal path. Years before, Ahab has lost his leg in pursuit of the whale. To get his revenge, he promises the crew riches if they land the beast. Vengeance, pride, and greed doom the ship. Ahab's overpowering and, ultimately futile desire to subdue the whale is an allegory about man's futile desire to dominate nature. Nature's power is too great. All but one of the crew drown as the ship is drawn into the vortex created as Moby Dick drags Ahab, strapped to him with a harpoon line, below the sea."

Here we have strong emotions (greed and pride) coupled with motive (vengeance) and psychotic behavior (obsession). Contrast these human traits with the indifference and power of the whale. Set them against the backdrop of the romance and mystery inspired by the sea. The result is a compelling premise that should intrigue the right editor—all done in thirty seconds.

Try this exercise on your own story. Here are the key points to remember:

─1. Start simply.

─2. Add descriptors that will transform your presentation into a compelling summary.

─3. Keep your audience—the editor—in mind at all times.

─4. Write your pitch to create a desire in the reader to see more.

─5. Don't add unnecessary detail; be succinct, but make the pitch irresistible.

Your story summary will be the basis for all your queries, discussions, and pitches to editors. Then, after you've captured an editor's eye, banked your advance, and submitted the final manuscript, when you need jacket copy that will have readers whipping your book off the shelves, you've got it right at your fingertips.

Melville, Herman. *Moby Dick.* Bantam Classics, 1981 (reissue), ISBN: 0553213113

Top Ten Reasons
Your Novel Gets Rejected

by Shirley Kennett

*T*ime after time your manuscript comes flying back, and you feel as though you're single-handedly supporting your local post office. There's no reason given, just another infuriating rejection letter—"Not right for us"—to add to your growing stack. It's time to take an objective look at your work.

Grab a cup of something warm and comforting, put your emotions in a place where they won't get in the way (the same place you store them when your least-favorite relatives announce they're coming for a two-week stay), take a deep breath, and go down the following list of reasons for rejections, culled from conversations with editors and agents. The reasons are arranged in rough order of importance, from least to greatest.

10. Your manuscript is not tightly edited and polished.

Incorrect grammar, spelling, and punctuation show you don't care enough to learn the mechanics of writing. Wordiness, awkward phrasing, and inappropriate word usage mark you as someone who needs to return to English Composition 101. Working with you in the future will be a continual clean-up process to bring your work up to the publisher's standards. Editors want manuscripts as clean as possible to reduce the cost of copy editing. Be brutally honest with yourself on this one. If you have a feeling your manuscript falls into this category, educate yourself. It's not beyond you. No one is born with dainty fingers curled around the *Chicago Manual of Style*.

9. Your characters are too autobiographical.

I call this the *poor me* syndrome. Many writers spend their first book or two working out personal issues. That's fine for your emotional well-being, but don't expect an editor to get excited about it unless your life story really is larger than life, or you are a celebrity. Most of us have lived mundane lives, which is one of the reasons we turn to fiction. You can use elements of your own life when creating characters, but use your imagination as well.

8. The pacing of your book leaves a lot to be desired.

If the editor's mind is allowed to wander, her body will follow, in the form of her fingers reaching for that rejection letter. The book should rise toward its climax through a series of plateaus. Action, intrigue, tension, or personal revelation build to a peak, followed by a breather. A breather happens when the protagonist is not actively involved in the main thrust of the plot. Breathers become shorter and shorter as the plot shifts into high gear. The interval between breathers gets longer as the book goes on, so that by the last fifty pages or so, there aren't any. Even if your book is character-driven and doesn't hinge on plot twists, it still should not be uniformly paced throughout.

7. You tell instead of show.

It's remarkable how easy it is to fall into that pattern. Many new writers take the shortcut of explaining a situation or backstory directly to the reader, spoon-feeding character development and plot events in neat swallows. Instead, show the action as it happens, letting the characters participate first hand in real time. A family argument can be told to the reader in a paragraph or two, but without emotional impact. If the scene is shown instead, played out in real time, all the reader's senses will be engaged. Which is more memorable?

6. You make too much use of stereotypes.

Use of stereotypical attributes is a shortcut to the preconceived notions of the reader. It's the easy way. All cops eat doughnuts and are gruff on the outside with a heart of gold inside; all college professors bumble around in dealing with everyday life. I do believe there's a place for stereotyping in good writing. The reason stereotypes exist is that they press buttons buried deep in the reader, with a predictable response. That might be just what you want from a particular character in your story. The problem is that it limits the reader's response to a narrow range of emotions. Most of your characters deserve more than that.

5. Your characters don't have strong motives for their actions, and are essentially pawns of the plot.

Actions don't spring from within the characters, but instead seem to be imposed on them. Even in plot-driven books, character motivation can't be ignored. Readers like to identify with one or more characters in a book, and they don't like to think of themselves as puppets. Weak motivation also leads to overuse of coincidences. Coincidences occurs in real life, but few readers will stick with a book that is rife with them.

4. Your story is padded.

Some publishers are interested in a particular word count, especially in genre writing. If a story doesn't sustain that length, don't pad it with inconsequential events. Some writers go so far as to take a concise phrase like "She was belligerent" and dilute it by saying "The woman seemed to be a little bit touchy, maybe even looking for a fight." Bingo, three words turned into fifteen. Add word count to a story by increasing the complexity of the plot, adding one or more meaningful subplots, or going into more depth in character development.

3. There is no "hook" at the beginning of your book.

The first five hundred words of your book are golden. That is the amount a browser might read in a bookstore as she examines your book. In those brief words, you must anchor the reader in a character, a situation, and a location. You must create enough interest for the reader to want to move deeper into the story. Don't rely on overused beginnings such as the dream, describing the weather, or having the character wake up and go through routine morning activities in detail.

2. *Your dialogue is stilted.*

Dialogue serves several purposes in your book. It is a wonderful tool for characterization, it can convey necessary information to the reader, and it breaks up dense writing. Dense writing means not having enough white space on the page, so that the passage looks like a textbook to the reader. Dialogue is a fast, exciting read during which the reader is fully engaged, and it may be as much as a third of your word count. Bad dialogue is an irritant from which the reader can't escape. Read your dialogue aloud— better yet, have a group of friends read it, acting out the passage, while you listen. If your characters are saying things so stiffly that the words would never come out of a real human's mouth, you've got work to do. On the other hand, dialogue is usually not a word-for-word representation of the way real people talk. It is condensed, more like the way we wish we could have said things. Your dialogue might be too ordinary.

1. *The voice of your book is simply not engaging.*

Voice is a combination of your protagonist's personality and your own writing style. Style consists of your word choice, sentence structure and length, tone, paragraph length, chapter structure, pacing, point of view, and probably a few things I missed. Editors are looking for a *fresh voice*, meaning something that is not a rehashing of other authors' work, something with genuine sizzle and a new way of looking at the human condition. On the other hand, many editors don't want something so far out that they fear it will have a limited readership. ("Limited readership" is not a tag you want to have applied to your book.) Search for a voice that plays on deep familiarities but explores new territory. That's a tough job, but no one said writing was easy.

If you've discovered that one of the above reasons for rejection applies to your writing, it may be the best thing that could happen to you. You can stop swimming around in that murky sea of not knowing why your work isn't making the grade, and focus on improvement. When you've conquered these top ten reasons for rejection, your book will stand out from the crowd, and be evaluated on its true strengths. Isn't that what you've hoped for all along?

I Am Your Editor:
Submitting Your Novel To Me

by Caro Clarke

I have been in publishing for over ten years, mostly as an editor. I am the person who accepts or rejects your manuscript. Here is how I make my decisions.

As I work my way down the slush pile, I look the envelopes I am opening. Sloppy presentation is not a good sign. Neat, clearly-labelled packages give me hope. I haven't even seen what's inside, and already I'm making judgements.

Out come the manuscripts. I check each one for a self-addressed return envelope with sufficient postage attached or with enough international postal reply coupons (if it comes from overseas). Is the SASE [self-addressed stamped envelope] big enough to hold the whole manuscript? Or is there a letter-size SASE for my reply? Good. I keep this submission on my desk. No SASE? I put the manuscript to one side. Maybe I'll read it. Probably I won't. I've had writers who have said: "You won't find an SASE here because you won't be rejecting this novel." Yes, I will. But he won't be seeing his manuscript again because I'm not paying to mail it back. I say goodbye to submissions without return addresses and submissions from overseas with their local postage attached. If the writer makes it too difficult or costly for me to contact him, believe me, I won't.

The submissions with proper SASEs are sorted again. Most rejections happen right then and, yes, I still haven't read a word of the text. Why do I reject them?

First, because the genre was not right. I've received children's picture books when I was working for a publisher of true crime. Didn't the writer check out our product? I've worked for a feminist press and received Clancy-style adventure novels for men. What did they expect? I've had science fiction when I was publishing poetry, poetry when I was editing short stories. What a waste of time, paper and postage. Specialist publishers do not publish outside their speciality. You won't be the exception.

Second, because the submission was not publishable. I have received one poem—and it was not in response to a call for an anthology. What did the poet expect me to do, write back saying "Gosh, such was the brilliance of this single poem that I ask—no, I beg—you to send me anything else you may have." That doesn't happen. I laugh and put it aside. It's not even a rejection. I have received manuscripts written in white ink on black paper. I have received photocopied manuscripts so faint I could hardly read the words. Believe me, I didn't read any. Do these writers think that their genius removes them from having to follow submission guidelines? That I'll be charmed by their funky individuality? Sorry, I'm a busy editor. Writers who don't make it very, very easy for me to understand what they're offering are begging to be rejected.

What makes it easy for me? First, a cover letter that tells me succinctly what the author is sending me. Something like this would do: "Please find enclosed my novel entitled *Blowing In The Wind*. It follows the struggles of a young actor to fight his cocaine addiction in order to win the heart of the scriptwriter he loves. It is a romantic comedy and will appeal to readers of *Postcards from the Edge*. It is 70,000 words." This pleases me. I know what I've got. Why would I reject at this stage? Usually because the genre is wrong, or we have too many of that kind of novel already. A pity, but that's life.

Those still on my desk get their cover letter read in full. There's still time for an author to head towards the rejection pile when I turn the page and look for a synopsis. None? I won't reject—yet—but I probably will. Also bad is the overly-long synopsis. I've been sent a fifty-page synopsis on a 200 page manuscript. It's a *synopsis*, for pity's sake. Two pages should be plenty. One page is even better. Or the synopsis might try to excite me with a cliff-hanger: "Ricky and Sandra are trapped in the car as it plummets in the ravine...and if you want to read the rest, you'll have to read the whole book!" No, Mr. Author, I'll have to reject you, mostly because anyone who tries to pique my interest this crudely will write this crudely. Goodbye.

I also enjoy the breathy cover letter that explains the psychology of the characters, the themes of the book, and the spiritual depths of the author: "This is a sensitive, brilliant, yet deep-felt novel exploring what it means to open yourself to the love that flows through the universe. The author is a reincarnated Hopi wise woman and offers deep mystical insights as the heroine becomes wife, mother, and shaman." Hey, who's the editor here? It's *my* job to decide if the novel is sensitive and brilliant. The author proposes, the editor disposes.

Now I have a much reduced pile of not-yet-rejected manuscripts. The cover letters on these are to the point, telling me what the submission is, what it is about, how long it is, what niche it fits into, and what its rivals are. Now I want to see what else the writer has done. I want to see a list of relevant other books or articles he's written. I'm all too familiar with the tricks writers use to disguise a thin portfolio, but having even one professional sale is important. They have a track record. It's not just my opinion against the world. What happens if there is no track record? Manuscript rejected? Not if I've been impressed with the writer's professional submission, but it does make me cautious.

My good opinion can still be lost at this stage if the submission has one or more of the following: a letter from the writer's pastor/mother/best friend/teacher/parole officer, telling me how much they enjoyed the enclosed book and recommending it to me; a photo of the author (when I want it, the publicity department will ask for it); a photo of the author's family, dog, pastor, favorite car, vacation; anything cute that's supposed to catch my eye and make me love the writer, such as felt animals stuck to the cover letter or manuscript, cookies, hand-made bookmarks, a prayer card, and so on; the manuscript itself tied together with ribbon, bound in any way (comb, spiral, glued into covers), decorated with bunnies and flowers (unless those are the illustrations). What kind of serious, self-respecting author would include such stuff? You think Toni Morrison sticks toy animals to her manuscripts? Please.

The submissions that passed through my first tests will have, besides a good cover letter and a polished synopsis, a manuscript clearly typed, double-spaced on one side only on standard white paper, with one-inch margins, pages numbered and with a running header that contains the author's name. The manuscript might be in a folder or a box or, better still, be the first three chapters clipped at the top left corner with a paper clip. I feel enmity towards any manuscript in a plastic folder or binder; they slither and can't be stacked. If I have a nice pile of cleanly typed pages, I am happy. It is at this point, and only at this point, that I start reading.

Scary, isn't it?

What do I read? Not cover to cover—I haven't the time. I read the first five pages. Does it grab me? Do I have any desire to read further? If so, I dip into the manuscript two or three places further in. Prose still of the same quality? Story seem to be moving along? Is the text clean, i.e., no typos or spelling mistakes, no clumsy re-typing? I might even skip to the last five pages and read those. Does the story seem to match the synopsis? Does it seem any good? Would our customers want to read this book? Can I imagine it having market out there?

I can't? Too bad. I reject it. If I'm not sure, I put it away to look at in my spare time, with a three-month deadline. I suspect I'll probably reject it then. I usually do. So no news is not always good news for a writer.

But hey, I've found one I love! I can't stop reading! I've read the first five pages, then fifty. I'm excited. I'll bring it to the editorial meeting, I'll fight for it, I might even get to publish it. This is what the professional side of writing is all about: making a no-gimmick, no-hassle submission that gets me to the point of reading. Why give me an excuse to say goodbye?

Nuts And Bolts

Punctuation/Grammar

> *Unless you're writing for a British publication
> (or for a U. K.-affiliated Canadian
> publication), punctuate according to standard
> North American English usage.*

Strange Punctuation

by Janis Butler Holm

Q:I'm confused about punctuation. In school I learned to punctuate one way, but some of the books I've read seem to be following a different set of rules. For example, I've seen single quotation marks where I was taught to use double, and I've seen the period at the end of the sentence placed outside, instead of inside, the quotation mark. What's going on here?

A: Were these books originally published in the U. K.? Many writers are unaware that North American English and British English have differences not only in spelling and meaning but also in punctuation. The examples you've given reflect popular British practice.

That is, most British publishers (but not all) place single quotation marks where we use double and double quotation marks where we use single.

British: Jane's look was one of disbelief. 'I cannot believe you have used the word "love" in this context.'

North American: Jane's look was one of disbelief. "I cannot believe you have used the word 'love' in this context."

Likewise, most British publishers require that quotation marks enclose *only* that material that is strictly a part of the quotation. If what is quoted does not itself include a period, the sentence period must go outside the quotation mark. But North Americans are taught to place a period inside the final quotation marks, whether or not the quoted material actually includes a period.

> *British:* He was forced to examine what he had actually meant by 'love'.

> *North American:* He was forced to examine what he had actually meant by "love."

When you're reading material published in the U. K., keep in mind that British punctuation practices are not uniform. Because British punctuation experts have differing views on the subject, writers and publishers in the U. K. have some flexibility in how they punctuate quotations.

Unless you're writing for a British publication (or for a U. K.-affiliated Canadian publication), punctuate according to standard North American English usage. When writing for a British publisher, punctuate according to the house style sheet.

Writing Exercises? Just Ducky

by Janis Butler Holm

Q:Some of the writers' sites I've seen on the Internet include writing exercises. Most of these look pretty silly to me—"Pretend you're a duck" and so forth. What's the rationale behind them?

A: Some writers are blessed with immediate expertise and a never-ending supply of creative energy. Most of us, however, are not. Most of us become writers through patience and practice, and writing exercises are, for many, a favorite form of practice.

Popular with both beginning writers who lack experience and experienced writers who like the occasional tune-up, writing exercises come in many forms. But a good exercise typically offers the following:

➤ a mildly structured task without the pressures of "real" work. The assignment encourages the writer to be relaxed, exploratory, and playful—to be less concerned with getting things right and more in tune with creative rhythms.

➤ a challenge to conventional habits of thought. The assignment invites the writer to move beyond his or her usual ways of seeing the world. It stretches the mind in new directions.

— an opportunity to learn more about what the writer *wants* to write. The assignment allows the writer to test a new subject or approach or personality without a major investment of time and energy. In a brief space, it offers the chance to discover an unexpected source of writing pleasure.

In short, good writing exercises can keep those creative juices flowing. They can lift us out of the humdrum and reveal our best writerly selves. But even the not-so-good exercise—the one that seems unbearably silly, for example—has something to offer:

— the opportunity to repeat the act of writing, which, like all physical acts, must be repeated in order to be mastered.

All writing exercises are a form of physical exercise; all of them help strengthen and refine that mysterious neuromuscular process by which we put words on paper or screen. But as with most forms of exercise, their impact is noticeable only after regular and sustained effort. The necessity of practice, of keeping pen to paper or hands to keyboard, is both the easiest and the hardest lesson that a writer must learn. Consider that time-honored truism: If you want to be a writer, write.

If you are interested in regular writing practice but not especially keen on investigating duckhood, try the more thoughtful exercises in Natalie Goldberg's *Wild Mind: Living The Writer's Life* or explore the list below. Or consider creating your own assignments. When all is said and done, it is not the assignment per se but what you make of it that really matters. Any topic will do, so long as it allows for invention, discovery, and surprise.

Bernays, Annie and Pamela Painter. *What If? Writing Exercises For Fiction Writers.* HarperCollins, 1995, ISBN 0-673-99002-8

Goldberg, Bonni. *Room To Write: Daily Invitations To A Writer's Life.* G. P. Putnam's Sons, 1996, ISBN 0-87477-825-5

Goldberg, Natalie. *Writing Down The Bones: Freeing The Writer Within.* Shambhala, 1986, ISBN 0-87773-375-9

Hodgins, Jack. *A Passion For Narrative: A Guide For Writing Fiction.* St. Martin's, 1994, ISBN 0-312-11042-1

Compound Words:
A Proofreading Pitfall

by Janis Butler Holm

You've eyeballed your copy, run your spelling checker program, and tested your friends' devotion by requiring them to read this latest masterpiece. Now you're ready to submit it for publication. Right?

Maybe. But are you sure about your spelling? What about those little problems that spelling checkers can't find? What about compound words that require hyphens? What about compound words that should be one word instead of two?

English spellings, though they sometimes follow simple rules ("I" before "E" except after "C," etc.), just as often reflect their accidental evolution in a living, changing language system. Or they may generally follow a set of logical principles, but the number of exceptions to those principles makes learning the rules an almost pointless exercise. Such is the case with the spellings for compound words, many of which defy our commonsense expectations of consistency. (Dictionaries give us "grandaunt" but "great-aunt," "hardheaded" but "hard-hearted," "night table" but "nightstand." We must "hand-feed" but "handpick," be "house-proud" but "house poor," spend a "half-dollar" or a "half hour.")

Recent editions of *The Chicago Manual of Style* include a fairly extensive set of rules for spelling compound words, a multipage reference chart that provides answers to any number of usage questions. Here we can find that noun + noun combinations are generally hyphenated ("author-critic," "city-state") and that the name for a "grand" relative is always spelled as one word ("grandniece," "grandfather"). We can learn that "quasi" noun compounds are spelled as two words ("quasi union," "quasi contract") but that adjectival "quasi" compounds are hyphenated ("quasi-judicial," "quasi-stellar"). However, other rules are more complex, and few writers will want to memorize the numerous guidelines that appear here in small print. And the lists of exceptions are not comprehensive, which means that, in many cases, the writer will need ultimately to consult a dictionary in order to be sure of the correct spelling.

To complicate matters further, Internet usage has generated a legion of new compound words. Though you can find these in various versions on the Net, lexicographers (dictionary editors) seem to be favoring one-word spellings, as in "cyberspace," "email," "homepage," "hyperlink," "newsgroup," "online," and "username." But they also seem to have settled on "Web site" instead of "website," so it is clear that the one-word form will have its exceptions. Just as for older compound words, careful writers will be checking their dictionaries.

Are there any shortcuts when it comes to checking compound word spellings? Given the frequency of compound words in English and their extraordinary variety, the answer is, unfortunately, no. Unless you have a day job as an orthographer, as a professional scholar of letters and spelling, the chances are good that you'll need to consult a dictionary when proofreading copy that includes compound words. While spelling checkers can find two-word compounds mistakenly written as one, and while orthographic rules can generate good guesses, the dictionary remains the best and final authority.

It's comforting to know that the good folks at Oxford have made an onerous job of linguistic selection just a wee bit easier.

The Infinitive: To Split or Not to Split?

by Bernard LoPinto

A great burden has been lifted from the shoulders of English language writers everywhere, and we have none other than the good people at Oxford to thank. A recent Associated Press article announces that the latest edition of the *Oxford Dictionary of the English Language* has repealed the interdiction against splitting infinitives. Praised be the name of Oxford.

Of course, this announcement has not come without a howl from certain quarters. According to the article, Loftus Jestin of Central Connecticut State University calls this seeming rule change an occasion for "great sadness...like listening to Mozart when the pianist keeps hitting all the wrong notes." (He must have been at one of my recitals.)

The article also quotes Samuel Pickering of the University of Connecticut (considered the inspiration for Robin Williams's character in *The Dead Poets Society*) as saying, "I do not dine with those who split infinitives." (Professor Pickering must be used to eating alone.)

The prohibition against splitting infinitives has little justification in English grammar, but it's one of those things we keep around out of respect for tradition. According to Morton Freeman, writer of *The Wordwatcher's Guide to Good Writing and Grammar*, the grammarian Fowler put the taboo to rest in 1926.

Strunk and White (*The Elements of Style*) trace the splitting of infinitives back to the fourteenth century, but White states that "the construction should be avoided unless the writer wishes to place unusual stress on the adverb." Later he writes, "The split infinitive is another trick of rhetoric in which the ear must be quicker than the handbook. Some infinitives seem to improve on being split...'I cannot bring myself to really like the fellow.' The sentence is relaxed, the meaning is clear, the violation is harmless and scarcely perceptible. Put the other way, the sentence becomes stiff, needlessly formal. A matter of ear."

Even the 14th edition of *The Chicago Manual of Style* is on board for this one, stating in a footnote that "the Press now regards the intelligent and discriminating use of the (split infinitive) as a legitimate form of expression and nothing writers or editors need feel uneasy about. Indeed, it seems to us that in many cases clarity and naturalness of expression are best served by a judicious splitting of infinitives."

Novelists strive for language that does not overshadow what we are trying to say. This puts us squarely between the traditionalists such as Pickering and Jestin, and a book-buying public that wants informal language.

It's comforting to know that the good folks at Oxford have made an onerous job of linguistic selection just a wee bit easier.

The Chicago Manual Of Style: The Essential Guide for Writers, Editors, and Publishers, 14th edition. University of Chicago Press, 1993, ISBN: 0226103897

Strunk, William, Jr. and White, E. B. *The Elements Of Style*, 4th edition. Allyn & Bacon, 2000, ISBN: 020530902X

Editing And Revising

Shape And Sharpen Your Fiction: Effective Revision

by Elizabeth Delisi

*T*here's nothing quite like the pride and feeling of accomplishment you get when you type the words "The End" on the last page of your manuscript. But once the euphoria passes, it's time to buckle down and to turn that wonderful creative project into something salable.

When you're writing a first draft, you're using your "left brain," the creative side, to draw on all your creative powers. Once your story is completed, let the manuscript sit for a while before you look at it again. This will give you the necessary distance from the material and allow you time to switch hats from "creator" to "editor."

Return to your material with a fresh perspective, and go over it with a critical eye. Reading aloud may help; you may also wish to solicit comments and suggestions from one or two trusted friends. Remember, though, that the ultimate responsibility for the manuscript is yours—don't take any suggestions unless you're sure they are sound.

The first thing to consider is your opening. This may be the most important part of your story; often, the first few paragraphs are all you have to "hook" the reader. Your opening must draw the reader's attention by introducing the main character and the main conflict. The reader should identify with the main character, and want to know more about the conflict and how it will be resolved. Rework your opening as many times as necessary to get it just right.

Think about your overall story. There must be movement, progression; the main character should change for the better or learn an important lesson by the end. Check your character descriptions and interactions to make sure it's clear what the reader is to think of each character, what the characters want, and what they care about. Be honest with yourself—do you, as a reader, care about the outcome of the story?

Be sure the climax you hint at in your opening actually comes about by the end of the story. Don't write a story with a big buildup that leads to a minor, disappointing climax. Tie up all your loose ends—don't drop unexplained hints or leave dangling story lines.

Include everything in the story that your reader needs to know. Remember, the reader doesn't have access to your in-depth knowledge of the characters and story—he knows only what you tell him. Don't leave too much to the reader's imagination.

Check your tone. Is it consistent throughout the story? If you start with a comic tone, then switch to tragic, it will seem as if two different people have done the writing. If you begin in present tense, don't switch to past in midstream. Use active rather than passive verbs. Consistency is also important in point of view. Don't switch from first to third person, or from third-person limited to third-person omniscient.

Make sure your most important scenes are fully fleshed out. They should usually be written in an action mode, with emphasis on dialogue and activity, rather than on description or exposition.

Look at your pacing. Does the story move too slowly or too quickly? When you reread it, do you find yourself skipping over sections? If you find a section that doesn't contribute to the whole, cut it out ruthlessly, no matter how beautifully written it is. Have you included too much information or too little? Does the story end in the right place? The reader should be satisfied with the ending—it should be logical, tie up all the loose ends, and flow directly from the story events.

Is your story organized properly? One way to check is to write a list of the major events in your story on index cards, with one event per card. Place them on the table or floor in the order in which they occur in your story. Then try rearranging them. Is there another sequence that makes more sense?

Check your transitions. For instance, if you have a flashback scene, is it clear to the reader that you are moving back in time? Transitions must be smooth yet also unmistakable.

When you've finished checking the creative aspects, check the technical ones. Use the dictionary, if necessary, to make sure your words are spelled properly. Don't rely on your computer's "spell check" feature—it can't tell the difference between "heel" and "heal," but that distinction will make a big difference in your story. Make sure you've used complete sentences and that your punctuation is correct. Look for repeated words—if you find you've used the word "finicky" twice in one paragraph, get out your thesaurus and find an alternative. Check your dialogue tags—make sure they're clear and unobtrusive.

After you've checked everything, let the story sit again for a few days, and then go through the entire process once more. When you're satisfied with the story as it stands, congratulate yourself for a job well done—and then send it out.

Overcoming Premature Revisionitis

by P. J. Woodside

Albert Camus, in his dark novel, *The Plague*, creates a character who has my deepest sympathy—a struggling writer hard at work on the greatest novel of all time (this despite the fact that the city is quarantined and that people are dying all around him). Almost every time we encounter him he's revising the first sentence. He believes that if he can get that beginning just right, the rest of the novel will fall into place.

The character never finishes his first sentence, much less the novel, and I always wonder whether Camus ever suffered from the same malaise. If he did, he overcame it with great success.

While some writers, especially new ones, have the problem of not revising enough, there are those of us with the opposite problem. I'll call it premature revisionitis. I suffered for years under the delusion that I was simply a good, close editor—never mind that I couldn't finish anything. Eventually, revision overtook creation, and I couldn't finish a single page for the desire to make it better, word by painful word.

Balancing these two impulses—the first to create; the second to fix—is the hardest thing about writing. First we must write without censor, allowing every tenuous connection to flow through the mind and onto paper. Then we must become the unsympathetic reader, the audience who knows nothing of our intentions, and slash our own precious words with sword and scalpel.

It is no easy balancing act. Revising too early makes no sense, like putting the doorknobs on a house before the walls and roof are finished. Not revising at all leaves a work with holes and bumps. We must be of two minds, but we must know which mind to use at which time.

Now that I've been writing half my life, I'm aware I must shut off the critic until I need her. This is no easy task, for my critic is sharp. She knows how to rearrange sentences for the most pronounced effect, how to cut passive verbs, wasteful adjectives, lowly "thats." She does not want to be silenced. She's the master.

And yet. . . and yet . . . what about this nagging little voice behind her, the one pushing from behind her skirts, the one with the story to tell. "Once this happened," it says, and the critic says, "That should be 'Once upon a time.'" The wee voice of the storyteller cannot get a word in edgewise if the critic will not shut up, at least temporarily.

My critic is the reason for four half-completed novels. She is the reason I never feel a story is quite polished enough to send out. She is also responsible for many well-wrought query letters—but if a query leads to a job, will she wait patiently for her turn at the manuscript?

She will, but only because I've learned a thing or two about this English teacher with a superiority complex who lives in my head. I've devised some methods of suppressing her until she's needed. Maybe one of these will help you.

1. Get into right-brain mode.

We are of two minds, which is exactly why writing is so difficult and yet so wonderful. Through left-brain processes (language, logic, organization) writing taps into right-brain territory (meaning, symbolism, imagination). Getting into right-brain mode helps you tap the dark, murky waters of the storyteller before the critic has a chance to censor and modify. In the past I have stared at a mandala for five minutes (no words, just shapes and lines), written letters (which tend to be less censored), or put on some Mozart. My husband rearranges his desk before he sits down. Currently I play Taipei on the computer. It's a short game that I can win (I'm not tempted to play again), and it consists of matching shapes (very right-brained). As soon as I'm done, I pull up whatever manuscript I'd planned to work on that day and begin.

2. Set goals.

When I'm working on the rough draft of a manuscript, I decide from the beginning approximately how many pages it should be. I write a minimum of four pages a day until I meet that goal. I might stop at some point in the process and do a bit of outlining, or move a scene or two around. But generally I just write, go with the flow, put down words. This is how I finished a middle reader (for ages 8-12) in six weeks, working a maximum of two hours a day. Revising took longer, but not nearly as long as if I'd tried to put the doorknobs on too soon.

3. Write more.

Are beginnings difficult? Write ten of them. One will inevitably lead somewhere. Ending hanging you up? Write ten endings. When you revise, you can decide what works and what doesn't. As for the middle, don't be afraid to change your mind in midstream. Later you might have to revise extensively, but that's easier than getting the flow back once you've interrupted it. For example, once I decided halfway through a novel that the situation in the beginning should have been slightly different. I wrote on as if it were. Only later did I actually change it.

4. Set limits on corrections.

Many writers find it hard to leave glaring spelling and punctuation errors behind as they type, but correcting them is a risk. I know I'm letting my critic out too soon, for example, if my eye starts to wander more than two lines up. Make quick changes if you must (throwing your critic a bone to keep her quiet), but set yourself a limit. And if you can go along typing at full speed despite the fact that you just wrote "jk;;oi" instead of "jackal," do so. Good luck figuring out what you meant. (That was my critic—see how nasty she can be?)

5. Let manuscripts cool.

Suppose you've managed to get a rough draft of a story finished. It's 2:00 AM when you finally crawl into bed. Next day, you wake with the excitement of the story in your bones. You want to read it, to see how wonderful it turned out. Take my advice—don't. You'll only be disappointed. Chances are, now that you've finished the creative side of it, your critic will take over and find all its faults at once, which is just too much rejection to handle during this honeymoon phase. Wait a couple of days, if you can. Or, as an exercise, write down all the elements of the story you think work well. When you do begin revision, keep your storyteller there behind the shoulder of your critic to remind her of what's important.

6. Avoid writers' groups.

I learned this one the hard way. Nobody except you knows what you mean in a story, and no one else can make it work. What do writers' groups have to do with your inner critic? Plenty. They either give her a bigger ego (catching other writers' obviously stupid mistakes) or cause her to overreact (thinking of all the ways to "fix" your story). Listening to others tear one's precious words apart hardly energizes a writer to rewrite successfully. Usually it drives a writer either to toss the story away or rewrite according to everyone else's suggestions, which never works. The harshest criticism I ever received made me angry enough to get better, but the getting better part happened while sitting at a typewriter, not on a couch in a writers' group. If you feel you must be in a group, if only to produce work and see what others produce, set a few ground rules—positive remarks only and perhaps discussion of technique. Better yet, join a readers' group. Reading what's actually being published is much more instructive—and more to the point.

7. Have children.

Okay, I'm just kidding about this one, but being with kids did loosen me up. It also exposed me to children's literature, which has freer reign in the imagination arena. I like that. My critic hates it. That's why it works.

Camus, Albert. *The Plague*. A. A. Knopf, 1948, ISBN 0679720219

I Can Always Spot A Beginner Because...

by Caro Clarke

As an editor, I know when I am reading someone's first novel. I have nicknames for the four give-away faults beginners make: *Walk and Chew Gum, Furry Dice, Tea, Vicar?* and *Styrofoam*. I see at least one of these in every manuscript where the author has not mastered the craft of writing before submitting his or her work. What are these four faults and, more importantly, how can you avoid them?

Walk and Chew Gum

The writer has not integrated action and dialogue, internal monologue and action, or internal monologue and dialogue. It is as if the characters can do only one thing at a time.

For instance:

> "If you think you're going to town you'd better think again," said Ralph.
>
> He put down his can of beer.
>
> "I'm not having any daughter of mine going to a Cantrell boy's party, and that's final!"
>
> "Oh, Pa! How could you be so cruel!" JoBeth cried.

Then, hunting in her pockets for a tissue, she dried her eyes and stared at him defiantly.

"If I want to go, how can you stop me?" she demanded.

Ralph had known this would happen. She had always been independent, like her mother. He half-lurched to his feet.

"You little hussy!" he bellowed.

Running up the stairs, JoBeth turned at the landing.

"I am going, do you hear? I am!"

Not integrating action and dialogue makes for jerky, lifeless prose. Combine, combine, always combine:

"If you think you're going to town, you'd better think again," Ralph snapped, putting down his can of beer. She was too damn much like her mother. "I'm not having any daughter of mine going to a Cantrell boy's party, and that's final!"

"Oh, Pa! How could you be so cruel!" JoBeth searched her pockets for a tissue, dried her eyes and stared at him defiantly. "If I want to go, how can you stop me?"

Ralph half-lurched to his feet, bellowing, "You little hussy!"

But JoBeth was already upstairs. "I am going, do you hear? I am!"

This might not be award-winning prose, but shows action, thought, and dialogue knitted together.

Furry Dice

Adjectives, adverbs, and prepositions are like furry dice hanging from a car's mirror. They don't do anything for the car's performance; they're simply clutter. I once stripped away a fifth of a novel's bulk by removing words and phrases such as "very," "up," "down," "over," "about," "some," "a little," "a bit," "somewhat," "whole," "just," and so on.

Let's see this in action:

She picked up the gun and aimed it straight at him. His smile disappeared as he lifted up his hands into the air. She waved him over to the wall, saying, "Spread 'em out, and no funny business, you hear?"

She checked all of his pockets for the money, then stepped back. "Okay, I'm convinced. You haven't got it."

This passage would be stronger with fewer modifiers, and tighter language, like so:

She snatched the gun and aimed. His smile disappeared as his hands went up. She waved him to the wall, saying, "Spread 'em, and no funny business, you hear?"

She checked his pockets for the money, then retreated. "Okay, I'm convinced. You don't have it."

Fifty-nine words have become forty-four and, even so, the passage could still be trimmed. Before you begin to rewrite, grab that net and remove those clogging, gratuitous modifiers that muddy the water. Hemingway didn't need them; you don't need them.

Tea, Vicar?

"More tea, Vicar?" Angela asked, taking his cup and placing it on the tray beside her.

"Don't mind if I do," said the Reverend Phelps.

"That was two sugars, wasn't it?" she queried, pouring the fragrant liquid from the heirloom pot into his cup and stirring in the milk. When he nodded, she dropped in two sugar lumps, stirred again, and handed him back the cup.

"Thank you, my dear," he said, accepting it with a smile.

How often have I read loving descriptions of cups of tea being poured, pots of coffee being made, even whole meals being cooked and eaten? Or of rooms cleaned or decorated, or journeys made? Too darn often. Writers get a high from conjuring a tableau out of thin air, and in the white heat of creation, they forget that tableaux of mundane details are not exciting. Readers will not share their euphoria. Reading about a cup of tea being poured is about as exciting as watching paint dry. How does this scene help further the plot or character development? It doesn't. The writer simply got carried away with description.

Fiction is supposed to be like life, but with the dull bits removed, not spelled out in excruciating detail. Examine your work. Test every scene. Is there anything that you think of as "setting the scene" or "capturing the atmosphere?" If there is, cut it. Every scene needs conflict and movement to give it life, and tea for the Vicar has neither.

Styrofoam

This is related to *Tea, Vicar?*, but it arises not from self-indulgence, but from panic. Styrofoam is the egregious padding novice writers stuff into their novels because they haven't enough story to tell (or think they don't) and want to increase word count. Padding is distinguishable because suddenly the forward movement of the story stops dead. Nothing happens for a few pages. I read, I read, and at the end I've learned nothing about the characters that I need to know, nor have the characters done anything essential to the story. Every scene should propel the plot to the crisis that will resolve the story by building character or action. Styrofoam does neither.

If you fear you haven't enough narrative, add more conflict. Don't give me tours of the countryside, long rambling chats, characters making travel arrangements, or any other lifeless blocks of prose. I want action. I want inexorable movement towards the crisis. I want to be gripped. So cut the padding. If that makes your novel too short, re-think your premise, your plot, your primary and secondary characters, and rewrite.

If you want your novel to be published, you'll have to eliminate these faults, because I, your editor, won't do it for you. I'll just send it back.

Your Novel Synopsis: Storming The Gates Of The Publishing Kingdom

by Joy Thompson

You've finished your first novel and feel certain it's destined for the New York Times bestseller list. You may be right. But in order to earn a place on that venerable list, you need to get your book published, and to get published you need an agent, publisher, or both. To get an agent or publisher, you need an act of God. An angel, posing as a respected author in your particular genre and happy to pitch your book on your behalf, might also do the trick.

While waiting for divine intervention, try the approach used by most unpublished novelists: send a scintillating synopsis of your book accompanied by a well-crafted query letter. It's certainly not as dramatic as a visit from a vision in white, but some agents and publishers will accept and even read your unsolicited letter and synopsis, thereby granting you an audience with the keepers of the gate to the promised land of publishing. Send them your unsolicited manuscript and your book will end up in the unpromising land of the slush pile. But these are the rules of the publishing kingdom, and you'd do well to learn and follow them.

A query letter describes your novel: its genre, length, and targeted market. A synopsis tells your novel's story in brief, attention-grabbing paragraphs. Think of your synopsis as the story description found on the back covers of paperback novels or the jacket flaps of hardbacks. Like tantalizing hors d'oeuvres, these descriptions are designed to whet your mental appetite in hopes that you'll order the main entree, or as is the case with authors, buy their book.

The synopsis is written in narrative form, present tense, and the point of view of your synopsis should match that of your novel. If your novel is written in first person, write your synopsis in first person. But whether in first or third person, the main function of your synopsis is to describe your story, emphasizing plot and characters. "It should accomplish three basic functions: state the premise of your novel, delineate and show motivation for the main characters, and detail the significant stages of plot development," says Phyllis Taylor Pianka in her book, *How To Write Romances.* (Writer's Digest Books, 1998). Although this is a how-to book for aspiring romance authors, Pianka's advice on writing a winning synopsis can be applied to novels of any genre.

In addition to your plot and main characters, the synopsis should provide a few basic details about the setting of your book. Where does it take place? Is your story futuristic, historical, or set in the present? Beyond the setting, what has just happened—or is about to happen—that will serve as the basis for the conflict of your story and affect the lives of your main characters? What is the conflict? And what are the key scenes?

As mentioned earlier, when it comes to writing a gripping synopsis, it helps to study those book covers. Take a look at how David Baldacci addresses many of the points listed above in the cover description of his New York Times bestseller, *Total Control*:

> Sidney Archer has the world. A husband she loves. A job at which she excels and a cherished young daughter. Then, as a plane plummets into the Virginia countryside, everything changes. And suddenly there is no one whom Sidney can trust.
>
> Jason Archer is a rising young executive at Triton Global, the world's leading technology conglomerate. Determined to give his family the best of everything, Archer has secretly entered into a deadly game. He is about to disappear—leaving behind a wife who must sort out his lies from his truths, an accident team that wants to know why

the plane he was ticketed on crashed, and a veteran FBI
agent who wants to know it all.

Unlike a cover description, your synopsis will give away your story's
ending. After the intensity of your conflict and key scenes, you'll want to
show how you resolve conflict and conclude your story, happily or otherwise. Plot twists need to be unraveled, mysteries solved, and characters settled
into some sort of stability and not left at gunpoint or on the verge of dying
from a life-threatening illness. Kill them or heal them—that's your choice
as author—but don't leave them in unresolved circumstances.

For many, the hardest part of writing a synopsis is the length. Reducing
your eighty-thousand-word novel into a few pages may seem like a daunt-
ing task. But remember, you aren't telling the whole story, just the highlights.
If it's not a main part of your plot, leave it out.

Your synopsis goes where you can't—right into the office and onto the
desk of a very busy agent or publisher. Once there, it needs to capture the
agent's attention immediately since there are almost certainly a few hundred or more packages just like yours sitting on that desk. In his book,
Literary Agents, Gary Larsen addresses the issue of synopsis length. "Agents
vary in how long a synopsis they prefer. A synopsis is an important selling
tool that, among other things, will be used to solicit interest in Hollywood,
where people don't read books," writes Larsen.

Chances are good that if you capture an agent or publisher's attention
with a short but riveting synopsis, they'll request sample chapters or your
entire manuscript. Remember that your synopsis is like an uninvited guest
in the agent or publisher's office. You want to make the agent glad you
dropped in. Just don't overstay your welcome.

Pianka, Phyllis Taylor. *How To Write Romances*. Writer's Digest Books, 1998 (Revised, updated), ISBN: 0898798671

Baldacci, David. *Total Control*. Warner Books, Inc., 1997, ISBN: 0446604844

Larsen, Gary. *Literary Agents: What They Do, How They Do It, and How to Find and Work with the Right One for You*. Revised and Expanded. John Wiley & Sons, Inc., 1996, ISBN: 047113046X

There are probably as many ways to approach editing as there are writers, but most successful writers develop a consistent editing "style."

Editing And Polishing Your Manuscript

by Eileen Alcorn Workman

Ninety percent of established agents will tell you that the most serious mistake new writers make is to submit manuscripts long before the work is polished enough to merit being marketed to publishers. This problem stems from a writer's eagerness to see his book in print. What most beginning writers don't realize (or don't want to believe) is that editors in New York are looking for reasons to reject most of what they read. So although the urge to "get it out" is strong, professional writers will resist the temptation. Instead, they devote enough time and energy to make certain their books will be taken seriously by the publishing world.

A number of authors have told me they put manuscripts aside for as long as six months before beginning the editing process. This delay enables them to detach emotionally from the work, which in turn allows them to "kill their darlings." This phrase (which you'll hear often) refers to deleting those wonderfully purple metaphors that sounded so good when the author was creating them but in retrospect seem silly or downright trite. If you wish to edit your novel immediately after completing your first draft, you'd best discipline yourself to detach emotionally from your words. Otherwise, those bizarre phrases and weird descriptions are likely to slip right past you during your edit and repel the very people they were designed to impress.

There are probably as many ways to approach editing as there are writers, but most successful writers develop a consistent editing "style." One that works well is what I call the Big Picture, Medium Picture, Small Picture approach to editing. This method calls for three major passes at the manuscript once the first draft is finished, each successive pass taking the writer through more nuanced and smaller-scale changes. This approach seems most logical and is also time effective, as it prevents a writer from agonizing over the placement of punctuation in a sentence that might not even appear once the final draft is completed.

The first pass, the Big-Picture edit, should be devoted to evaluating the plot. Read the novel from cover to cover and take notes on the flow of your story. Does your central conflict begin early (within the first five or so pages) and rise consistently throughout? Have you interspersed your expository scenes and character descriptions with blocks of action so as not to bore your reader? Does the novel say what you envisioned when you began the writing process? How dramatic is the tension, and does it reach a crescendo at the story's climax? Have you finished each chapter with a scene that will inspire your reader to turn another page?

Once you've considered these questions, it's time to begin editing your novel by beefing up the thin spots and deleting those sections that do nothing to forward your story. During this plot pass, correct any lapses in logic that make your tale seem implausible. In addition, allow yourself to consider alternative plot twists. Can you create more tension by having a character perform act B instead of act A (as it was written in the first draft)? If so, then by all means rewrite the scene.

Now that you've answered the above questions, it's time for the Medium-Picture pass. On this read, you should more closely examine your characters and dialogue. Do your characters behave in consistent fashion, based on the way you've created them? Are they interesting? Do their actions and words accurately reflect who they are and what they are about? When they speak, do their speech patterns and word choices match their age, education, and background? Does every line of dialogue forward the story, create tension, or better define a character or the setting? Addressing these questions can make the difference between a ho-hum novel and a terrific book. Below is an example of dialogue/character behavior that has been edited to punch up a story dramatically:

Draft One:

Eliza, I've looked everywhere for the children. They're not in the den or their beds. Where are they?"   .

"Mrs. Carpenter, you're not going to believe this." I handed her the dusty leather book. "Christine found this book of magic spells in an old trunk in the attic, and decided to try and cast one. Suddenly...poof! They were gone."

Draft Two:

"Oh my god, the children! Eliza, they're missing. What happened?"

I couldn't look at her. My hands shook as I held out the ancient and dusty leather book Christine had found in the attic. I wished with all my heart we'd never opened that awful old trunk.

Christine's mother glanced at the book and frowned. "What's this? Eliza, tell me this instant. Where are my children?"

I swallowed hard. "Do you believe in magic, Mrs. Carpenter?"

Draft One, while technically adequate, answers the important questions as soon as they're asked. Draft Two tantalizes the reader by raising additional questions. This approach increases the tension and pulls the reader more deeply into the story.

Having considered character and dialogue, you should now be ready to make your Small-Picture pass. This read is for grammar, punctuation, syntax, and clarity. Are your commas, semicolons, and colons appropriately placed? Do your modifiers (the few you've allowed to remain) accurately describe your nouns and verbs? Did you use the correct word— "farther or further," "either or neither," "lay or lie"? Did you use the exact word to say what you meant, or did you settle for a close-but-not-quite substitute? Have you varied your sentence structure so that the book doesn't read with a tiresome sameness but instead moves forward in a snappy, interesting fashion? Have you killed all your darlings, or are there still a few loose-cannon metaphors out there that seem sillier now that you've read them over several times?

Be brutal. Be honest. Be professional. And if in doubt, be wise enough to set the book aside and try again another day. Above all, promise yourself you won't mail your manuscript until you're 110 percent convinced you've written the cleanest, sharpest, most enjoyable book you can.

Criticism/Rejection

The Most Important Writing Lessons

by P. J. Woodside

For a long time I believed writing would be easy if I just figured out the tricks. I spent years in writing classes taking notes, rearranging sentences, crossing out adjectives, changing points of view, and grappling with plot. The real lessons, though, the ones that changed me, were more difficult, more complicated, and seldom welcome.

The first lesson: rejection is necessary. All writers must deal with criticism, and the worst comes from the people you admire the most. In college, where I first studied with published writers, I wanted nothing more than to be in their ranks. I hung on their every word. I lived and breathed by their compliments.

And I died by their criticism—or felt I did. For in those years when each word from my pen seemed sacred and hallowed, their criticism cut to the heart. Could I take the blows? Could I survive the rejection? I found the answer to be a long and exasperated *yes.* The criticism hurt, but it also made me become a better writer. It forced me up over a wall that might have blocked me longer had I not been pushed.

At least those first writer-teachers believed in my talent. Not so with my next one. He was a much more accomplished writer who didn't coddle or praise or even notice his students very much. And, oh, how we wanted his notice. One student had been taken under his wing—groomed, introduced to an agent and published in a prestigious literary magazine. The rest of us yearned to be next in line, submitting stories so polished and wonderful that we felt sure our genius would be recognized. It didn't happen—not for me, at least. Instead, this nationally acclaimed writer, for whom I still have great respect, wrote me a letter of recommendation that said I had only modest writing ability. Talk about a blow to the ego!

This kind of rejection is much harder to take, for it discredits not a particular piece of writing but one's very ability to write. We've all heard of now-famous writers who were told at some point in their careers that they didn't have the talent of a stick. They survived those blows, but could I? Could I believe in myself enough to keep writing in spite of the opinion of one who should know?

To add insult to injury, I then received rejections from several of the writing programs to which I'd applied. That's when I made a vow to quit writing. It was my lowest moment, but I found out something important. I couldn't quit! Every time I told myself I'd never write again, that I'd never put pen to paper for the purpose of creating literature, this little voice in the back of my mind answered, "Yes you will. You *will*." It taunted me. It haunted me. It pushed me over the wall.

Here, then, is the second lesson I learned: not everyone will believe in my ability. In the real world, most work will be rejected by most editors. I needed to believe in myself if I hoped to publish, despite the doubts of others.

I finally made it into a good writing program, where I learned my next lesson. The full-time and visiting writers critiquing my work sometimes couldn't agree on the most basic rudiments of writing. They emphasized opposing elements. They contradicted themselves. Some of them didn't even like each other.

Did I learn about writing? Yes. But, more importantly, I learned I must make choices, for there is no one way to be a writer. I also learned something about commitment, which I believe is essential to good writing. Though I respected my various teachers for various reasons, the one I admired the most spent the least time working with his students. His writing came first—always, no compromise. And that, I realized, was because of his commitment. He lived, ate, and breathed writing.

Other students in the program complained about him. They wanted to be encouraged, advised—taught, for heaven's sake. But if they'd been paying attention, they would have realized writing cannot be taught. It can only be shown. The rest is up to the writer, which is what our teacher so aptly demonstrated.

I received a degree eight years ago, but since that time I've been learning continuously—about discipline, self-reliance, hard work, and sacrifice. There are no tricks. Though my studies taught me a lot about writing, classes could not make a writer out of me. Writing made a writer out of me. And that is the most important lesson of all.

*Good writing is full of language
that is simple but
powerful in imagery.*

Nobody's Perfect:
Guidelines For Critiquers
And The Critiqued

by Sunnye Tiedemann

*I*f you're shy about critiquing others' work because you feel inexperienced, don't be. You are a reader, and you know what you like. Just so you won't get lost in your own insecurity, here are some suggestions to help you get started.

First, both the critiquer and the critiquee have certain responsibilities.

Critiquer: Be constructive. Critique unto others as you would have them critique unto you. Saying you like or don't like something is not critiquing; you must say what you think should be done to make it right. Concrete suggestions to improve the story are always helpful.

Critiquee: Submit polished work for critiquing. No rough drafts, please. Bring a current manuscript. Submit only your own work.

How Should the Critiquer critique?

Step 1. Read the story all the way through, without stopping. (Ignore mistakes, concentrate on the story.)

Step 2. Reread the manuscript and, on either a separate paper or on your copy, note all strengths and all weaknesses. (You may or may not use all of these in your final critique, but don't let any escape your eye.)

Here are some things to consider:

The Title:
> Is it appropriate?
> Does it pique your interest?
> Does it hint at the story without giving too much away?

The Story:
> How is it written?
> Does the author show the story, as opposed to telling it?
> Is the beginning effective?
> Does the first paragraph hook you?
> Do early paragraphs get you into the story immediately, introduce the main character, hint at conflict?
> How fast does it move?
> What's the conflict?
> Is the climax effective?
> Does the story end quickly and satisfactorily?

The Characters:
> Are they clearly drawn?
> Do story events change the main character?
> Is there enough description of characters and their actions so that you can tell them apart?
> Is each character's dialogue distinctive so that you can easily tell which characters are speaking and/or acting at different times?
> Does the main character have a past? Is a future implied?
> Can you spot character tags?

The Language of the Story:
> Are sentences rich in strong verbs and nouns, or are they filled with cliches and unnecessary adjectives and adverbs?
> On the other hand, is the writing pedestrian and journalistic?
> Good writing is full of language that is simple but powerful

in imagery. Some adjectives are necessary, but these can be easily overdone—your instinct will help here.

Are there mistakes in grammar?
>Is the author consistent in using verb tenses?
>Do all pronouns agree with antecedents?
>Does the author use similes and metaphors to enrich the language
>of the story without overdoing it?
>Are similes and metaphors appropriate to the subject matter?

The Setting:
>Are scenes adequately described so that the reader knows where the action takes place?

The Structure:
>Does the story read smoothly?
>Do events occur logically?
>Does the plot develop with credibility? (That is, do events motivate characters sometimes and other times do characters create events? A story must grow from its own action, and character motivation must be consistent.)
>Is there a beginning, middle, and end?
>Is viewpoint consistent?
>Are transitions clear and logical?

The Style:
>Is the mood consistent with the kind of story?
>Does the author use too many cliches?
>Is there authorial intrusion in the story?
>Does the story sag in the middle or fizzle at the end?
>Is the writing clear? If you find hazy sentence structure, point it out and suggest a correction.

The Ending:
>Is it powerful, logical, and clear?
>Does the story end at the right place?

When you critique, sandwich praise and criticism, always ending your critique with words of encouragement.

Critique the writing, not the subject or any opinions the author may express. Give your reaction to the story, as well as what you liked and didn't like.

Concentrate on structure, content, character development, and storytelling rather than on grammar and mechanics, but gently point out any consistent grammatical errors because good spelling and good grammar *do* count with editors, as do properly submitted formats and little things like SASEs!

How should the Critiquee respond?

Don't argue. You don't have to explain anything (if you have to explain, it's not clear enough in the manuscript), but you may want to discuss points the critiquer has made. Do so. Carefully consider all suggestions.

Be as objective as you can.

Put some distance between you and your story. Criticism of the story is not criticism of you as a writer; it is criticism of the methods you've used—there may be some better way that you didn't know about.

Remember: When all is said and done, it's your story, and *you* make the final decisions. Remember that the purpose of critiquing is to help you improve your work, learn your craft, grow in professionalism, and, most of all, help you get published.

Last: Remember to have a good time while you learn.

The Talent For Accepting Criticism

by Rodney Lewis Merrill

*A*re writers born or made? Can someone teach you to write, or
must you be born with talent? I've never heard a compelling
answer.

Given my own experience, I would say that writing can improve greatly
with coaching and teaching. Am I naturally slicker with words or more
creative than average? I don't know. I can say only this much with certainty:
When I compare my coached final drafts with the "before" versions, it's like
comparing a banquet to garbage.

If facility with words can be cultivated by coached practice, then the
ability to stand away from your work may be just as important as writing
aptitude. A good writing coach, if given the freedom, can anticipate snares
and misunderstandings. (What you "mean to say" has little significance if
readers think you mean something else or they're too bored to care what
you mean.)

I once labored for three weeks, fine-tuning a personal essay before hand-
ing it to my reader. I imagined that she would respond to my work
dramatically, dabbing at her eyes, stammering and sobbing while she searched
in vain for the right words to tell me it was the most touching thing she had
ever read. Instead, her eyes glazed over as she turned the first page. A pained
squint came over her by page four. She struggled to read page five but then
excused herself, feigning a migraine instead.

That's hard to take. When people you know find fault with your inner-most thoughts and feelings, it is easy to conclude that the fault they find is with you. Their response can feel like betrayal—as though they are really saying, "I've just realized what a fatuous ass and complete waste of space you are." But behaving as though your mentors and critical readers are Judases encourages neither honesty nor willingness on their part. When they sense that your easily bruised ego doesn't distinguish the message from the messenger or assistance from assassination, people will flee your com-pany. Or they'll say only nice things about your work. Or they'll pretend to have a migraine.

Believe me, I understand the difficulty of taking criticism graciously—I'm easily bruised, temperamental, and prone to feelings of dejection and abandonment. Dan, my former writing instructor, once said something that seemed to help. He had marked up my manuscript so badly that it looked like rush hour roadkill, then scrawled this P.S. across the bottom: "Hey, I'm a lot better at peddling this shit than following it. But it's true just the same."

Somebody say "Amen."

References

*If you are still using white-out to correct your
mistakes on screen, you probably need
the "introduction to personal computers"
course, as well.*

Tools Of The Trade: Six Essential Items For The Modern Writer

by Gwenneth Barnes

I s there anything computers can't do these days? If you're a writer, this question probably sounds absurd. Let's rephrase it. Is there anything you're currently doing that your computer could do just as well—or possibly better?

Computers are great for doing mindless, repetitive work. They free up the author's mind for more consequential things, such as figuring out how a romantic heroine will win the heart of her magically enabled lover and live happily ever after on the jeweled gas clouds of Planet Pflorg.

With a reasonably capable computer and a well-chosen set of tools to go with it, you can hand off some of the more tedious tasks to your computer. This enables you to get on with more creative aspects of your writing. (By the way, our heroine does finally get the attention of her beloved, and, together, they create dozens of beautifully embossed trilogies of gas-cloud children with a knack for solving murders.)

Here's what you need to make all your characters' wishes come true. In some cases I'll mention products by name, but do realize that most of the time there are equally good substitutes to try before you buy. Don't be afraid to get specific recommendations from people who know what they're talking about.

Some of the items I'll recommend may seem extravagant—certainly, some of the tools would be perfectly at home in the network server room at a high-tech software company. But if you make your living as a writer, or spend your off-hours writing the ultimate novel, doesn't it make sense to use the best tools you can afford?

The six items that belong in the well-equipped writer's tool kit are:

1. Good word processing software

My personal favorite is Microsoft Word, but there are many others out there that are equally capable. Your word processor should be able to proof-read your text; apply automatic page numbering; add headers and footers to your manuscripts; and calculate and insert page, word, and character counts.

The most powerful word processor in the universe is not going to do you much good if you use it the same way you would use a typewriter, though. Invest some time in a night-school course on how to use your chosen software. You'll not only learn how to make your margins and page numbering come out right, you'll also find out why you shouldn't hit the Enter key at the end of every line.

If you are still using white-out to correct your mistakes on screen, you probably need the "introduction to personal computers" course, as well.

One seldom-observed rule with powerful software is "never go with the 'point-oh' version of anything if you can help it." New releases of large programs tend to be buggy, so let others crash-test it for a few months before you upgrade. By the time you buy, there will be patches or "service packs" available to fix the problems reported by the "early adopters."

2. A decent printer

Personal laser printers are competing favorably with ink-jet printers these days, and usually produce cleaner, sharper output. Your printer should be capable of creating crisp, clear print on ordinary paper, at a respectable rate of speed. Printing a twenty-page chapter should not require you to load the printer with paper and retire for the evening.

Ink-jet printers are economical, but the ink can smudge or even run if it gets wet, and the ink cartridges can be messy to handle. Some require special paper, and some are painfully slow. Color ink-jet printers are virtually useless for manuscripts. Editors won't be impressed with multi-colored type, and you have up to four ink cartridges to deal with instead of just one.

Dot-matrix printers are good for printing ten foot-long "HAPPY BIRTHDAY" banners but not much else. Editors dislike dot-matrix output and often won't accept it. Spend the extra bucks for a laser printer if you can, or put your manuscript on a floppy disk and take it to your local copy shop (Kinkos, for instance) for quality output and short-term cost savings.

3. A reference library on CD-ROM

Skip the multimedia encyclopedias with full-screen video and surround-sound for this selection. Head straight for *Microsoft Bookshelf.* This title is updated yearly, so if you're on a budget, check the bargain bins or the swap meet for last year's version. The information doesn't go out of date as quickly as Microsoft would like you to believe.

On the disk you'll find a dictionary, a thesaurus, a book of quotations, and a smattering of other reference books that change year by year.

If you've ever browsed through a paper dictionary to see what story ideas pop into your head (you have, admit it), you will find the hyperlinked references in *Microsoft Bookshelf* completely enthralling. This is especially true when a name leads to a quotation, which leads to a reference to another quotation, which leads to a list of links to encyclopedia entries and from there into an oblivion even sweeter than that caused by a gallon of chocolate ripple ice cream.

Don't be tempted, however, to use the World Wide Web as a substitute for a CD-ROM based reference library—it is far too easy to get sidetracked for hours at a time on the web instead of working. The web is a useful tool, but it's also a world-class time waster that should be reserved for nonwork hours only.

4. A backup system

This should really be at the top of your shopping list because it's so important. Sooner or later, your hard drive will crash. In fact, some experts claim that with hard-drive prices falling, manufacturers are starting to use cheaper, less reliable parts to cut costs. This cost-cutting has ominous imcations for the shelf life of your precious manuscripts if you don't make regular backups.

Choose tape, ZIP disks or other compact, high-capacity removable media, and make regular backups. I'll say it again: Make regular backups. There is no sight known to humanity, or to help-desk staff, more pathetic than an author who has just lost a year's work because of a hard-drive failure.

Implement a backup routine you will actually use. Copying the contents of your 3.6 gigabyte hard drive onto AOL startup diskettes is ridiculous. You won't do it more than once, I guarantee it. Meanwhile your hard drive is heading inexorably towards its Mean Time Between Failures. When failure occurs, your files will suddenly (or, worse, slowly and undetectably) become garbled beyond repair, then vanish entirely.

The ideal backup system is one that works whether you remember to use it or not. Next best is something simple and quick. Tape drives are easier to use and somewhat more reliable than they used to be, but few backup methods are more convenient than those 100-megabyte (or 250-megabyte) ZIP drives. There are other removable media with similar capacity, some that even use a drive that can read regular 3.5-inch floppy disks. Also consider investing in a CD-ROM burner for your backups.

Network administrators, whose jobs depend on being able to rescue files when users delete them accidentally or hard drives crash, recommend keeping three sets of backup media and using them in rotation. Store one set of backups in a remote location in case your office succumbs to fire, burglary, or other disaster.

Losing your Beanie Baby collection to a flash flood is bad enough. Having to recreate a book-length manuscript from memory is something altogether worse.

5. A UPS (Uninterruptible Power Supply)

This may sound like more of a techno-weenie toy than a writer's tool, but a small investment in power protection can save you thousands in burnt hardware and lost work if lightning strikes nearby or your local electrical utility decides to treat you to a rolling blackout.

Don't rely on "surge protector" power strips. They may protect you once from a power surge, but after that they function as multiple electrical outlets that offer no more protection than a cheap extension cord.

A UPS has an internal battery that is constantly being charged up by the current from your wall outlet. This battery gives you a few minutes to shut everything down gracefully if the neighbor's teenager backs the family car into a power pole and blacks out the neighborhood.

On better UPSs, the devices you plug into the UPS actually run from the battery rather than from the electricity in your walls. This provides smoother, more consistent voltage to your expensive equipment—low-voltage "sags" can be just as harmful to electronics as spikes or surges.

Some UPSs even work in conjunction with your computer's operating system to shut down all your programs automatically, even if you're not there when the lights go out. It won't be the most fun you ever had spending money, but you'll be glad you did it when the unthinkable happens.

6. A PIM (Personal Information Manager)

This is not just an electronic address book. Yes, you'll use it to keep track of editors and publishers who might be markets for your manuscripts, but you'll also be able to keep records of what went where, when, and to whom.

The information can be useful at tax time, particularly if you need to prove that your writing is a home business with legitimate deductions for postage and office supplies. If you're conscientious about updating your data regularly, your PIM will have all the information you need to make that nice tax collector go away and leave you alone for another year.

The PIM tools that come with Microsoft Outlook, for instance, include a calendar, an address book, a task list, a journal that links to files you've opened recently, and, of course, an email client. You can get Outlook bundled in some versions of the Microsoft Office Suite.

If your writing is generating income, Quicken is a great tool for managing your business and keeping track of cash flow. Because you can store your contacts as vendors and customers, you can also use Quicken to manage your address list.

Yes, there are contact-management and manuscript-tracking programs made specifically for writers, and some are good enough to be useful. But they don't do anything a PIM can't do for you, and a PIM is useful for storing other things besides manuscript- tracking information—for instance, names and addresses of all your friends and relations, or even your characters

Does this list add up to a big chunk o' change? You bet. Do you have to buy everything on it at once? No way. Is your life's work worth it? Only you can decide that.

The Thesaurus—Writer's Friend or Foe?

by Janis Butler Holm

Q: I've found my thesaurus really helpful when I'm looking for just the right word, the one that simply won't come to mind even though I know it's out there. But I've been told that using a thesaurus can stunt my growth as a writer. How so?

A: The thesaurus, or synonym-finder, is a wonderful tool, teeming with the riches of the English language. As you are happily aware, in a thesaurus one can find what the French call "le mot juste"—the exact word, the expression that best embodies what one wants to say. As does a good dictionary, a good thesaurus can help writers communicate more clearly and efficiently. It can help make writing more precise, more accurate, and sometimes more effectively nuanced.

In itself, the thesaurus poses no threat to a writer's development; it has no inherent growth-stunting properties. But, like all good things, it can be misused. Beginning writers, in particular, can easily become too dependent on this writer's aid, such that they lose confidence in their own ability to generate the right words. And some novice authors use a thesaurus to find exotic terms that they think sound sophisticated and highly intellectual, sometimes with disastrous effects.

Typically, writers who use the thesaurus wisely are those who feel comfortable with their own writing voices, who look for more effective synonyms only in the editing process or when specific problems arise, and who can recognize when a word does or does not seem natural to their vocabulary. In short, they put their own words first.

What are the danger signs for misuse? You will want to reconsider your relationship to your thesaurus if

> ⸚ your writing has slowed to a snail's pace because you look for synonyms before you've sketched out a good draft,

> ⸚ you're using the thesaurus to dress up your natural diction with flashier words, or

> ⸚ you no longer feel you can write without a book of synonyms at hand.

All of these situations suggest a lack of confidence in writing, and confidence can be built only through thinking and working in one's own words. As experienced writers are well aware, the key to writing success is a well-developed personal voice, something no thesaurus can provide.

A word of caution: It's usually wise to find one style manual, get familiar with it, and stick with it.

Why We Need Style Manuals

by Ann Meeker Beardsley

Style manuals began as simple guidelines for newspapers and general interest magazine publishers. Because they had a large and varied audience, editors had a vested interest in keeping the prose simple and easily understood. Where space was valuable, editors encouraged writers to use commas sparingly. They wanted shorter sentences and avoided the use of semi-colons and colons, which tended to lead toward longer sentences and, therefore, longer articles. Literary novels, however, catered to readers who enjoyed reading elaborate sentences and had the time to parse out convoluted paragraphs. Complex punctuation—such as those same semi-colons and colons—made long sentences more readable.

Writers who switched from one format to the other needed guidelines, so publishing houses and newspapers developed their own in-house rules for how to handle the myriad choices that made their publication different from the others. Eventually, those style choices were published in employee manuals, and then in style manuals available to the public.

Those differences still prevail in today's publishing world. Newspapers use simpler structures, literary novels are (generally) much more complex, and popular novels rest somewhere in between. While choosing the wrong style manual for your work won't mean automatic rejection by an unfeeling editor, choosing the right style manual won't raise any flags or editors' eyebrows. But how do you choose?

First, evaluate your own writing. Are you aiming for the newspaper market? There's the *Associated Press Stylebook And Libel Manual*, used by many newspapers. Some newspapers—like the New York Times—have their own widely available manual, which is (almost, but not quite) like the *Associated Press Stylebook*. Writing a novel? Find out what manual the publisher you're aiming for is using. Chances are, it's the *Chicago Manual Of Style*, 14th edition. But keep in mind that there are literally hundreds of style manuals to choose from. The only thing they all have in common is that they require (yes, require) consistency.

Here's a short list of stylebooks you might want to consider:

The Associated Press Stylebook And Libel Manual
More people write for the Associated Press than for any other single newspaper, so their style manual carries a lot of clout. It is extremely easy to use; most entries are alphabetical. The manual has special sections for sports and business writing, and an extensive libel reference. AP has recently branched out and now publishes separate manuals for broadcasting, sports, and photojournalism.

The Chicago Manual Of Style, 14th edition
Published by the University of Chicago, this manual is a standard in the book publishing industry, and is particularly suited to literary works and long scholarly texts. However, it's big and very complex. A review of its past publication history shows that it's revised about once every ten years; the last revision was in 1993.

The Elements Of Style, 4th edition
Written by William Strunk Jr. and E. B. White, this book has been around a long time and is an excellent self-guided tour of proper English language usage. It ought to be required reading for high school students as it gives a thorough grounding in most basics. Unfortunately, it doesn't get into the fine detail that most writers are seeking.

Publication Manual Of The American Psychological Association, 5th edition.
If you're writing a dissertation or other scholarly material, this manual is usually required. Special sections deal with organization, headings, and

references. Not quite as complex as the *Chicago Manual Of Style*, but it's still a hefty resource at 400 pages and it covers all the basics.

MLA Style Manual And Guide To Scholarly Publishing, 2nd edition.
This book is a popular source for high schools and colleges, and has extensive information on theses, dissertations, and citations, including Web sources. Easy to use, but not as much detailed information as some of the other style manuals.

As you search for a style manual, keep in mind that it's important to find the latest edition. Because it was written in 1993, the *Chicago Manual Of Style* doesn't give explicit information for citing Web sources. One presumes that the next edition, when published, will cover such information. Don't give up hope if you have a previous edition, though—websites are sometimes updated much more frequently and may answer your questions.

A word of caution: It's usually wise to find one style manual, get familiar with it, and stick with it. Because of the inconsistencies among style manuals, trying to remember whether or not to use or a comma or spell out the number 10 can take a tremendous amount of time away from doing what you should be doing—writing. Don't let delving into style manuals be excuse #371 why you can't write today.

Goldstein, Norm. *The Associated Press Stylebook And Libel Manual.* Perseus Publishing, 2002 (Revised and updated), ISBN: 0738207403

The Chicago Manual Of Style: The Essential Guide For Writers, Editors, and Publishers, 14th edition. University of Chicago Press, 1993, ISBN: 0226103897

Strunk, William, Jr. and White, E. B. *The Elements Of Style,* 4th edition. Allyn & Bacon, 2000, ISBN: 020530902X

Publication Manual Of The American Psychological Association, 5th edition. American Psychological Association, 2001, ISBN: 1557987912

Gibaldi, Joseph. *MLA Style Manual And Guide to Scholarly Publishing,* 2nd edition. Modern Language Association of America, 1998, ISBN: 0873526996

Authors' Biographies

Authors' Biographies

Bridget Anderson's writing career began in 1987 when she moved to Atlanta, Georgia. She has published six novels for BET/Arabesque books, the latest being, *All Because Of You*, May 2002. Bridget has spoken at several writer's conferences including: Moonlight & Magnolia, Atlanta, GA; Memphis Black Writer's Conference, Memphis, TN; Duel On The Delta Writer's Conference, Memphis, TN; and Writing in the LowCountry, Beaufort, S.C.
Email: banders319@aol.com

Laura Bagby is a writer and artist. She has an M.A. in English. She has written for and taught for Novel Advice for several years. For over five years she has taught accredited online university courses. She has published many poems short stories and articles. Currently she has a published novel, *The Perfect Man*, which can be ordered online or through major bookstores. She is working on a non-fiction book and two novels.

Gwenneth Barnes is a technical writer and artist living in California. Gwen's professional background includes fiction and nonfiction writing, technical documentation, radio and print journalism, web site development, graphic design and fine art.

Ann Beardsley is a freelance copyeditor for several major publishers and journals and a writer for several national magazines. She teaches self-editing to small groups near her home in Charlotte, NC. Ann is also a longtime contributor to NovelAdvice, a frequent book reviewer for Scribesworld.com, and is working on her first suspense novel and two nonfiction reference books.

Peggy Ullman Bell resides on the Mississippi Gulf Coast, but she lives in cyberspace where she hosts the Novel Ideas Workshop on AOL, and manages her extensive website. A former columnist for NovelAdvice, and an award-winning poet in her own right, Peggy's fictionalized biography of the poet Sappho has been selected as required reading in Women's Studies programs at several renowned universities. Peggy's second novel features the Battle of Gettysburg.

 Email: peggyullmanbell@cableone.net
 Website: http://www.peggyullmanbell.com

Victoria Harnish Benson is a columnist for Hawaii's *Punahou Bulletin*, and has been published in numerous Internet magazines. She is a contributing author for *Chicken Soup for the Volunteer Soul*, 2002, and has a published book, *To No Man's Glory: A Child's Journey From Holocaust to Healing*. Mrs. Benson recently turned to screenwriting and editing.

 Email: WrytRyt@aol.com

Tricia Bush lives in Upstate New York. She has been a staff writer for Novel Advice for several years and currently co-hosts a writing workshop on AOL. She is an avid reader and occasionally edits novels for friends. She is widely traveled, first as a military "brat" then 26 years as a military wife. Tricia is a graduate of Denison University and has lived and traveled extensively in Europe. She has directed plays, written music, and paints "intermittently".

 Email: Tbushpurr@aol.com

Caro Clarke is the author of the novel *The Wolf Ticket* and has written short stories for several small literary magazines. She is also a published poet. A Canadian, she now makes her home in London, England, where she has worked in publishing and for authors' rights organizations, and now works on the internet. She has been writing for NovelAdvice since 1998.

 Website: http://www.mallet.dircon.co.uk

Elizabeth Delisi is the author of three novels, two short story anthologies, and three novellas. She also edits for small publishers and for individuals. Delisi is a staff writer at NovelAdvice and a columnist at Word Museum. She teaches writing classes at NovelAdvice, Word Museum, and Writers Online Workshops and she has taught creative writing at the community college level.

 E-mail: delisi@ruraltel.net
 Website: http://www.elizabethdelisi.com

Wendy Walton Dickerman, a passionate wordslinger since the fifth grade, lives in Oregon. She has written two books of poetry; one completed and two in-progress novels; hysterically nearing completion of a nonfiction book for women (*Permission To Breathe, Finding Your Voice and Claiming a Joyful Life: Meditations and Battle Strategies*), not yet published. Wendy has drawers full of poetry, articles, a screenplay, and altruistic fantasy notions. She also wrote for NovelAdvice for over four years.

    Email: WindLEO@aol.com

Joy V. Formy-Duval lives on the history-rich southern coast of North Carolina. Since she began serious writing in 1992, many of her poems and several short stories have been published. Her goal is to be published in book length in her favorite genres of romance and mystery. She is a member of Mystery Writers of America, Sisters-in-Crime and Romance Writers of America.

    Email: Loveajoy@aol.com

Gwendoline Y. Fortune (Gwen) has written most of her life. Her first "composition" was the lyrics for her high school class song. Newspaper columns, academic writing during an earlier incarnation as Professor of Social Science/History and classical singer led to current hectic promotion for her first novel, *Growing Up Nigger Rich*, Pelican Pub. (2002). As a poet (from a singing-dancing-instrumentalist—background), who writes beyond genre, Gwen loves weaving words. Her second novel is with the publisher, the third is in process, and she has plans for more.

    Website: http://zenarts.com/GUNR/

Jeremiah Gilbert is a graduate of the University of California and currently teaches at two southern California colleges. His first collection of poems, *In a Strange Land*, is forthcoming from Mellen Poetry Press.

    Website: http://www.jeremiahgilbert.com

C.J. Hannah was born, raised, and educated in Colorado and recently returned there after thirty-seven years in California. He is the author of several novels, the newest of which is *Midnight Writers*, coming out next summer. He is the founder of the Asilomar Writer's Consortium 25 years ago which is still going strong. He was a workshop leader at Santa Barbara Writers Conference for seven years and has been a workshop leader for Southern

Califorinia Writer's Conference in San Diego for the last 15 + years. He is also a workshop leader for Southern Califorinia Writer's Conference in Oxnard.

Janis Butler Holm writes and teaches in Athens, Ohio. She attributes her love of language to her mom, Lee Butler, and sometimes collaborates with her sister, Bett Butler, who is a jazz columnist.

Shirley Kennett has published five novels. Her latest is *Burning Rose*, published by Five Star Mysteries in March 2002.She puts her extensive computer background to use, but the technology never overwhelms the characters—or the reader. She is a member of the Mystery Writers of America, Sisters in Crime, and the American Crime Writers League. Kennett teaches online writing courses and edits queries, synopses, and opening chapters. She lives with her husband, sons, and cats in St. Louis.

Email: shirleyk@shirleykennett.com
Website: http://www.shirleykennett.com

Marcia Kiser writes, works and lives in Lubbock, TX. She is a member of Sisters in Crime, the Palo Duro Chapter of NSDAR and was a contributing editor to Murderous Intent Mystery Magazine. Pubications include Without A Clue, Murderous Intent Mystery Magazine, Nefarious, Mysterical-E, *Futures*, Mystery & Suspense Zine, and Over My Dead Body. She is currently hard at work on various short stories and nonfiction articles.

Email: Mek357@aol.com

Rose P. Lee lives in Arizona. She is a graduate of De Paul University. Rose published her first story at the age of eight. Since then, she has published books and over 500 articles and short stories. Rose enjoys writing about modern southwestern Native Americans. She has published factual tales of Eastern Europeans arriving in the United States 1900-1910. She has taught college writing classes, writing seminars, and workshops.

Email: Katkeys@aol.com

Bernard LoPinto, a life-long writing teacher, has been honored to share his often singular ideas about the English language with NovelAdvice. His writing and photography have been seen in various publications in

New York State, and he has recently turned his hand to the short story. Bernard lives with his wife Jeanne, a few turtles and fish, and some frogs.

Email: lasteagle@yahoo.com

Rodney Lewis Merrill has over 400 articles and reprints to his credit. These encompass a wide range of subjects, including reviews of books, magazines, e-zines, and educational media; personal essay and nature essay; poetry; and feature length articles on distance education, biomedical ethics, health and fitness, environmental issues, practical psychology, rural living skills, and cooking. Rodney lives in Astoria, Oregon, where he operates DegreeFinders, a consulting service that assists clients in researching and evaluating distance learning degree programs.

Email: rlmerrill@charter.net
Web site: http://www.DegreeFinders.com/

John Moir has published a nonfiction book and many articles, stories, and columns. He has also won a number of national writing awards. John writes for several magazines and is also working on a mystery novel. He lives in Santa Cruz, CA, but someday wants to be one of those authors who describe themselves as "dividing their time" between fabulously exotic locales.

E-mail: John@jmoir.com

Karen Oberst lives in Washington State. She has been writing regularly for Novel Advice since March 1998, and has also written and published four books. Oberst's alter ego is the Quote Lady, and she can be contacted at her Web site devoted to inspirational quotations.

Website: http://www.QuoteLady.com

Sheldon Reiffenstein is a business owner, and a writer in his spare time. As a freelance writer for business, he has helped various companies, large and small, develop persuasive communications to customers. As a business owner, he strives to create and sell products that answer a customer's age-old question, "How will your product or service benefit me?" He is often seen riding in elevators.

Email: sheldon@morethanwords.us

Joy Thompson is a freelance writer and author of one unpublished novel. Her articles, columns, essays, and short stories have appeared in numerous online and print publications. A certified Kripalu yoga instructor, she currently divides her time between teaching yoga, writing, and work on a second novel. She lives in Hampton, VA with her husband and two cats.

Email: joyforyoga@hotmail.com

Sunnye Tiedemann, aka Ruth Fulton Tiedemann, is a writer/photographer whose book reviews, short stories and articles have appeared in nationwide magazines, newspapers and online. She taught writing at the college/adult education level for 15 years. She and her husband are currently raising their four grandchildren in the Nebraska woods while she writes their memoirs and learns HTML.

Email: sunnye@sunnyetiedemann.com
Website: http://www.sunnyetiedemann.com

Amy Kay Watson is the author and publisher of A Bowl of Writers' Cereal. She lives in Ohio with her husband and two cats, and is currently writing a crime of deception novel called *The Engineer*. She recently served as an editor for her sister Barbara Watson for her book *Wake Up Barbara, and Help Me Find This Snake!*

Website:http://www.geocities.com/amykaywat/

P.J. Woodside currently lives in Kentucky, where she and her husband combine writing and teaching careers. She has recently begun her second novel and is marketing the first, a coming-of-age story set in the turbulent early 70s about a confused teenager and the women who influence her life.

Email: all4pj@charter.net

Eileen Alcorn Workman is a published short story and nonfiction author who is currently completing a collection of short stories. She has written four novels and taught numerous plotting workshops via the Novel Advice program. A financial consultant by day, she writes at night alongside her aspiring novelist husband, David. They live on a working avocado ranch in the hills above Malibu, California.

Email: eileenla@aol.com
Website: http://www.writeperfect.com

Recommended Reading for Writers

Compiled by Lin Mouat,
Novel Advice Bookstore Manager,
and Jeanne Marie Childe, Editor

Note: A few of these books are out-of-print, but are still available at used bookstores and online at http://half.ebay.com, http://www.powells.com/, and other sites.

Berg, Elizabeth. *Escaping into the Open: The Art of Writing True.* Harper Perennial, 2000, ISBN: 0060929294

Browne, Renni. Dave King. *Self-Editing for Fiction Writers.* HarperCollins, 1994, ISBN: 0062720465

Cameron, Julia. *The Vein of Gold: A Journey to Your Creative Heart.* J. P. Tarcher, 1997, ISBN: 0874778794

Checkoway, Julie, ed. *Creating Fiction.* Story Press, 2001, ISBN: 1884910513

Conrad, Barnaby. *The Complete Guide to Writing Fiction.* Writers Digest Books, 1990, ISBN: 0898793955

Frey, James N. *How to Write a Damn Good Novel.* St. Martin's Press, 1987, ISBN: 0312010443 (Other books by James N. Frey include: *How to Write a Damn Good Novel, II: Advanced Techniques for Dramatic Storytelling* and *The Key: How to Write Damn Good Fiction Using the Power of Myth.*)

Gardner, John. *The Art of Fiction: Notes on Craft for Young Writers.* Vintage Books, 1991 (reissue), ISBN: 0679734031

Gerard, Philip. *Writing a Book That Makes a Difference.* Story Press, 2002, ISBN: 1884910564

Hall, Oakley M. *The Art and Craft of Novel Writing.* Story Press, 1994 (reprint), ASIN: 1884910025

Heffron, Jack. *The Writer's Idea Book.* Writers Digest Books, 2000, ISBN: 0898798736

Henry, Laurie. *The Novelist's Notebook.* Story Press, 2002, ISBN: 1884910424

Johnson, Bill. *A Story Is a Promise: Good Things to Know Before You Write That Screenplay, Novel, or Play.* Blue Heron Publishing, 2000, ISBN: 0936085614

Keyes, Ralph. *The Courage to Write: How Writers Transcend Fear.* Henry Holt, 1996 (paper), ISBN: 0805031898

Lamott, Ann. *Bird by Bird : Some Instructions on Writing and Life.* Anchor, 1995, ISBN: 0385480016

Leland, Christopher T. *Creative Writer's Style Guide: Rules and Advice for Writing Fiction and Creative Nonfiction.* Story Press, 2002, ISBN: 1884910556

Lukeman, Noah. *The Plot Thickens: 8 Ways to Bring Fiction to Life.* St. Martin's Press, 2002, ISBN: 0312284675

Maass, Donald. *Writing the Breakout Novel.* Writers Digest Books, 2001, ISBN: 0898799953

Marshall, Evan. *The Marshall Plan for Novel Writing: A 16-Step Program Guaranteed to Take You from Idea to Completed Manuscript.* Writers Digest Books, 2001, ISBN: 1582970629

Marshall, Evan. *The Marshall Plan Workbook : Writing Your Novel from Start to Finish.* Writers Digest Books, 2001, ISBN: 1582970599

McClanahan, Rebecca. *Word Painting: A Guide to Writing More Descriptively.* Writers Digest Books, 2000, ISBN: 1582970254

Morrell, David. *Lessons from a Lifetime of Writing: A Novelist Looks at His Craft.* Writers Digest Books, 2002, ISBN: 1582971439

Novakovich, Josip. *Fiction Writer's Workshop.* Story Press, 1995, ISBN: 1884910033

Novakovich, Josip. *Writing Fiction Step by Step.* Story Press, 1998, ISBN: 1884910351

Perry, Susan K. *Writing in Flow: Keys to Enhanced Creativity.* Writers Digest Books, 1999, ASIN: 0898799295

Rico, Gabriele Lusser. *Writing the Natural Way: Using Right Brain Techniques to Release Your Expressive Powers.* J. P. Tarcher, 1983, ASIN: 0874772362

Sharp, Caroline and Elizabeth Gilbert. *A Writer's Workbook: Daily Exercises for the Writing Life.* Griffin Trade Paperback, 2002, ISBN: 031228621X

Shoup, Barbara and Margaret Love Denman. *Novel Ideas: Contemporary Authors.* Alpha Books, 2001, ISBN: 0028640683

Stein, Sol. *How to Grow a Novel: The Most Common Mistakes Writers Make and How to Overcome Them.* St. Martin's Press, 2002, ISBN: 0312267495

Stern, Jerome. *Making Shapely Fiction.* W.W. Norton Company, Inc,, 2000, ISBN: 039332124X

Wood, Monica. *The Pocket Muse*. Writers Digest Books, 2002, ISBN: 1582971420

Zinsser, William Knowlton. *On Writing Well: The Classic Guide to Writing Nonfiction*. Harperreference, 1998, ISBN: 0062735233

Printed in the United States
832400003B